McCARTHY AND THE COMMUNISTS

THE CHALLENGE OF TRADITION

Democracy is still upon its trial. The civic genius of our people is its only bulwark, and neither laws nor monuments, neither battleships nor public libraries, nor great newspapers, nor booming stocks; neither mechanical invention nor political adroitness, nor churches nor universities nor civil service examinations can save us from degeneration if the inner mystery be lost. That mystery . . . consists in nothing but two common habits. . . . One of them is the habit of trained and disciplined good temper toward the opposite party when it fairly wins its innings. . . . The other is that of fierce and merciless resentment toward every man or set of men who break the public peace.

WILLIAM JAMES (1897)

McCARTHY and
the COMMUNISTS

JAMES RORTY and MOSHE DECTER

GREENWOOD PRESS, PUBLISHERS
WESTPORT, CONNECTICUT

Library of Congress Cataloging in Publication Data

Rorty, James, 1890-
    McCarthy and the Communists.

    1. McCarthy, Joseph Raymond, 1908-1957. 2. Com-
munism--U. S.--1917-   3. Internal security--U. S.
I. Decter, Moshe, joint author. II. Title.
⌐E748.M143R6 1972⌐   973.918'0924 ⌐B⌐   78-138179
ISBN 0-8371-5636-X

Reprinted in 1972 by Greenwood Press, Inc.,
51 Riverside Avenue, Westport, CT 06880

Library of Congress catalog card number 78-138179
ISBN 0-8371-5636-X

Printed in the United States of America

10 9 8 7 6 5 4 3 2

Contents

ACKNOWLEDGMENT

The officers of the American Committee for Cultural Freedom wish to express their appreciation to the several score artists, scholars, scientists, and businessmen whose support made this study possible.

Preface

Public opinion in the United States has been polarized by the methods and consequences of Senator Joseph McCarthy's campaign against Communism in the United States. Because we are troubled by the fact that the heat of the McCarthy controversy has, for good and bad reasons alike, diverted attention from the most morally reprehensible and militarily dangerous threat to freedom now facing America, the American Committee for Cultural Freedom initiated this study as a public service.

The intention of this book is clear: to ascertain the facts about Senator McCarthy's campaign against Communism, to analyze its implications for American security, and to focus attention on constructive ways for supporting the national interest. The task is educational rather than political. In a sense we are seeking responsible answers to four questions:

What are proper criteria for judging the effectiveness of any anti-Communist campaign?

How do the methods and consequences of Senator McCarthy's campaign measure up to these criteria?

What has been the impact of the McCarthy controversy on traditional American values?

Where should we go from here in meeting the security problem posed by the Communist conspiracy?

In sponsoring this book, the A.C.C.F. believes it is exercising its necessary responsibility of bringing clarity and insight to the definition of crucial national issues, particularly those in which the cultural freedom of Americans has been directly threatened.

The Committee is an active association of leaders of the American cultural community in the fields of literature, art, music, philosophy, education, and the social and physical sciences. Affiliated with similar organizations in England, France, West Germany,

Italy, Latin America, India, Japan, and elsewhere in the world, the American Committee has devoted most of its efforts to rallying intellectuals here and abroad in a responsible, serious, and persistent struggle against all forms of totalitarianism, especially Communism — the greatest present threat to democratic communities.

The American Committee for Cultural Freedom, which includes individuals with points of view representing all parts of the political spectrum compatible with democracy, wishes to associate itself most strongly with the intent of this study, but the Committee does not assume responsibility for the facts stated or necessarily endorse all opinions expressed. These matters are quite properly the responsibility of the individual authors, in whose competence and integrity the Committee has the greatest confidence. The Committee also wishes to dissociate itself from the approval or disapproval of specific recommendations for legislation made by the authors of this volume. The organization, under the terms of its franchise, cannot make such recommendations; but it does not wish to prevent the authors from calling attention to legislative proposals which, in the authors' opinion, would help to resolve some of the difficulties they discuss.

ROBERT GORHAM DAVIS
Chairman

GEORGE S. COUNTS
Past Chairman

SOL STEIN
Executive Director

American Committee for Cultural Freedom
35 West 53rd Street
New York 19, N. Y.

McCARTHY AND THE COMMUNISTS

1. The Divided Front Against Communism

Under the continuous pressure of Soviet aggression, the temper of American unity against Communism has hardened steadily since the end of World War II.

There is no real disagreement or confusion among our people about the necessity of resisting Communist military and diplomatic aggrandizement abroad, or of exposing and suppressing Communist espionage and subversion in the United States.

There *is* disagreement and division over a man and an "ism": Senator Joseph R. McCarthy and the phenomenon that has been called "McCarthyism."

In this division the Communist Party finds rich opportunities for the achievement of its aims: to confuse and alienate our allies; to obscure the role of the Communist Party as a conspiracy; to blur the differences between Communists on the one hand and liberals and democratic socialists on the other; to create a new United Front of civil-libertarians against McCarthyism as an allegedly greater menace than Communism, thereby diverting and neutralizing the energies of the free world that should be channeled instead into the prosecution of the Cold War.

National unity is desperately needed if we are to discharge the responsibilities of free-world leadership that devolve upon us. And national unity is precisely what the Communist Party dreads more than anything else. A perusal of the Communist *Daily Worker* would reveal that the strategy of the Party line is, as it has always been, to confuse, to divide, and ultimately to weaken and sap the strength of this nation.

In 1954 the American people spent weeks in fascinated absorption, watching the televised hearings of the Senate Permanent Subcommittee on Investigations, in which Senator McCarthy and the Department of the Army leveled charges and counter-charges against each other. Did McCarthy and his staff — as the Army contended — seek preferential treatment for Private G. David

1

Schine? Or did the Army — as McCarthy contended — use Schine as a "hostage" to prevent the continuation of the McCarthy investigation of alleged Communists at Fort Monmouth?

One may question whether these are really the issues that transfixed a national audience before its television and radio sets. Is the American public primarily concerned with who blackmailed whom, with who told the truth and who committed perjury? Does it really care so vitally who shined Schine's shoes? If it does, then perhaps the whole special investigation may really have been a waste of time.

The audience could not tear itself away from the hearings because in them it sensed all the ingredients of a great psychological, political, and constitutional drama. It caught a glimpse of characters and motivations in conflict, of a great intramural struggle for power in the Republican Party, of a constitutional conflict of interest between the power of the Legislative Branch and the prerogatives of the Executive Branch.

Over and beyond these inherently exciting developments, the Army-McCarthy imbroglio represented for the American public the symbolic culmination of the great controversy that has raged about the Junior Senator from Wisconsin since the evening in 1950 when he strode onto the stage of an auditorium at Wheeling, West Virginia, waved a sheaf of papers at his audience, and began a speech that was to make him one of the most applauded — and most denounced — politicians in the world.

Since that time, Senator McCarthy has become for many Americans "Mr. Anti-Communist," the one dedicated scourge of Communism in or out of government. For others he is a dangerous, power-hungry demagogue, whose activities have had the net effect of helping rather than hurting the Communist cause.

His partisans see him as the vigorous statesman whose revelations have alerted the people to the dangers of Communist infiltration, whose singlehanded pressure was responsible for the tightening up of government security procedures, and whose methods, admittedly rough, are nevertheless indispensable for rooting Communists and loyalty risks out of government.

His opponents, on the other hand, view him as a demagogue whose methods parallel those of the Communists, whose revelations have been irresponsible or untrue, and whose contributions to the national security, whatever they may have been, are wholly disproportionate to their cost in terms of national disunity and the encouragement of an atmosphere hostile to democracy.

The controversy has been the greatest single factor contributing to the bitter partisanship of the debate about Communist infiltration of our government and to the embittered atmosphere that has in some measure driven reason, restraint, and persuasion from the national scene.

These have been the terms of the controversy. But why all the furor?

Surely there are more than enough staggering problems that warrant Great Debates without the McCarthy controversy: How should we conduct our Cold War strategy? How are we to handle the awesome power of the H-bomb? What shall be our policy in Southeast Asia? What must be the limitations and commitments of our foreign policy? And — yes — how are we to safeguard our internal security? These are all Great Debates that should be conducted soberly and rationally.

But instead of this kind of Great Debate, we have been diverted into a frenetic and noisy argument that has produced recrimination, mutual doubt, and suspicion. Partisanship and intense feeling are rife — despite the pleas of President Eisenhower for calmness and unity.

If we can still the uproar and lay gently but firmly to rest the controversy about Senator McCarthy, we can then hope to take the issue of Communism out of politics and meet it as a nation determined.

Why, then, have we allowed ourselves to be diverted from the truly Great Debates to this frenzied squabble? What, in reality, has been Senator McCarthy's role in the fight against Communism? What historical factors made possible his role and the controversy about it?

The American people emerged from World War II with kindly sentiments toward our "great wartime ally," the Soviet Union, and with the hope that the sacrifices of the war would be followed by an era of peace, good will, and reconstruction. But, as Vice President Nixon put it on November 18, 1953, "We had misjudged the intentions of the Soviet leaders." In 1945 Moscow openly repudiated the Grand Alliance (which the Kremlin's generals and diplomats had covertly sabotaged even before the war ended). Our hopes and illusions were shattered in short order by a new kind of "diplomacy" — the Cold War.

It was not that there had been no voices clearly warning us of the nature of the international Communist conspiracy to subvert the free world. There had been — years before Senator McCarthy entered upon the scene. But they were voices in the wilderness. Most Americans did not care until the stark facts were thrust upon them.[1] They had forgotten the lessons of the 1939 Stalin-Hitler pact.

There followed a rapid series of events that made it crystal clear that the Soviet Union had not abandoned its plans for world domination. The daily newspapers brought the shocking news home to Americans, as the tide of Red imperialism flowed into the power vacuum created by the defeat of the Axis powers and the premature withdrawal of America's armed forces. In a few short years during and after the war, the Soviet Union swallowed up Rumania, Bulgaria, Yugoslavia, Albania, and then Poland and Czechoslovakia.

But, once faced with this new threat, the free world slowly began to unlimber and to resist. In 1947 was enunciated the Truman Doctrine, under which American military and economic aid ultimately helped to defeat the attempted Communist coup in Greece and to strengthen Turkey's resistance to Soviet encroachment. In the same year the French and Italian coalition governments threw out their Communist contingents. In 1948 the Marshall Plan began to bolster the economies of all the free European nations. And in 1949 the North Atlantic Treaty Organization was formed, engineered by Secretary Acheson with bipartisan support.

But at the same time that the United States was thrust into the position of leader of the free-world coalition, its people were confused as to how to handle the threat of Communist subversion inside the United States.

In 1948 and 1949 the nation followed the political drama in which Alger Hiss and Whittaker Chambers starred as principals. At the conclusion of the drama (two weeks before Senator McCarthy embarked on his anti-Communist campaign) Hiss was sentenced to five years in a federal penitentiary — legally as a perjurer, implicitly as a proven traitor to the United States.

The effect of the Hiss case on the American people was electric. Moreover the fears aroused by the revelations of the case and by the growing Soviet threat were intensified by the disastrous course

---

[1] During the 1930's and early 1940's, some members of the American Committee for Cultural Freedom were hooted from public platforms, abused in print, and considered eccentrics by their government for opposing Communist brutality as strongly as Nazi brutality, Soviet slave labor as strongly as Nazi slave labor, Stalinist totalitarianism as strongly as Nazi totalitarianism — all at a time when friendship toward the U.S.S.R. was fashionable. It is difficult to forgive apologists for Buchenwald. It is just as difficult to forgive apologists for Kolyma — which still exists.

of events in the Far East. The Chinese Communists, with the Kremlin's help, were moving toward control of the vast Chinese mainland, and we seemed helpless to do anything about it.

Indeed, President Roosevelt's concessions to Stalin at Yalta proved to have calamitous consequences for China. Furthermore, a later Senate investigation led by Senator McCarran demonstrated that, at the time, a combination of deliberate and unwitting misinterpretation of the Chinese Communist movement and of the Kuomintang had misled many of our State Department Far East policy-makers into considering Mao's forces as harmless "agrarian reformers." One of these experts, John Stewart Service, admitted he had turned over classified state papers in 1945 to the editors of the pro-Communist magazine *Amerasia*. He was suspended — and then *reinstated in government service.*

All of these events gave rise to the growing fear of Communist infiltration and to increasing demands that the danger of Communist subversion be handled in a systematic and thoroughgoing way.

For Americans there was indeed real ground for apprehension. Communists and their sympathizers had actually nested in many government agencies. They had arrived in Washington early, during the first years of the New Deal, and had dug themselves deep into both the newly created alphabetical agencies and the old-line departments. They rose high and stayed late.

The House Un-American Activities Committee under its first chairman, Martin Dies, had named some of them during the 1930's. But Dies made the mistake[2] of lumping Communists together with liberals and welfare-state socialists who abhorred all totalitarianisms, including Communism. On the other hand many of the New Deal liberals were equally careless in their cries of "witch-hunt."[3] In their indiscriminate denunciation of Dies & Company, they defended alike the innocent, the dupes, and the guilty.

Yet we know now that as early as 1935 Communist infiltration of sensitive areas of government was well advanced. The overwhelming weight of evidence before the McCarran committee, for

[2] Most strikingly in Appendix IX of the Report of the Special Committee on Un-American Activities [Dies Committee], House of Representatives, 78th Congress, 2nd Session, 1944, called "Communist Front Organizations [etc.]."

[3] It cannot be pointed out too often that "witch-hunting" is a most inappropriate designation for the campaign against Communist infiltration. Witches, after all, never existed; but Soviet agents unfortunately are all too real.

example, was that among those who served the Communist conspiracy in the 1930's and 1940's were:

(1) An executive assistant to the President: Lauchlin Currie.

(2) An Assistant Secretary of the Treasury: Harry Dexter White.

(3) The director of the Office of Special Political Affairs in the State Department: Alger Hiss.

(4) The secretary of the International Monetary Fund: Frank Coe.

(5) The chief of the Latin American Division of the Office of Strategic Services: Maurice Halperin.

(6) A member of the National Labor Relations Board: Edwin S. Smith.

(7) The chief counsel of the Senate Subcommittee on Civil Liberties: John J. Abt.

(8) The chief of the Statistical Analysis Branch of the War Production Board: Victor Perlo.

(9) A U.S. Treasury attaché in China: Solomon Adler.

(10) The Treasury Department representative and adviser in the Financial Control Division of the North African Economic Board in UNRRA, and at the meeting of the Foreign Ministers Council in Moscow in 1947: Harold Glasser.

(11) The director of the National Research Project of the Works Progress Administration: David Weintraub.

These men and scores of others like them were described, in sworn statements to the FBI by Whittaker Chambers in 1943 and by Elizabeth Bentley in 1945, as members of Communist espionage rings.

Thus by 1945, when the Kremlin had shown its hand and the Cold War was on, the Democratic administration had in its possession all the data it needed to justify a thorough overhauling of the haphazard and incomplete security measures that had been adopted before and during World War II.

What were these early measures and how did they work out in terms of our internal security? They were of two kinds:- legislative and administrative.

1. Legislative measures

Beginning in 1939 Congress passed the following measures designed to keep Communists out of government:

(a) 1939: Emergency Relief Act, prohibiting payment of

funds to any "member of an organization that advocates the overthrow of the government of United States by force and violence."

(b) 1939: Hatch Act, making it illegal for any government employee to be a member of such an organization.

(c) 1941: Emergency Ship Construction Act, making it illegal for subversives to receive government wages. (This provision has become part of every Congressional appropriation bill since then.)

(d) 1946: McCarran rider to the State Department appropriation bill, authorizing the Secretary of State to dismiss any employee "whenever he shall deem such termination necessary or advisable in the interest of the United States." During the war, Congress had similarly authorized the military departments to dismiss any person for "conduct inimical to the public interest in the defense program of the United States." (By 1950, the Navy had fired 244 persons, the Army 115, and the Air Force 9 — all of them civilians, since the law did not cover service personnel.)

There were undoubtedly others who, as a result of Congressional impetus, were either kept off the government rolls or dismissed. But the inertia and automatic defensiveness of government officials, coupled with the muddled thinking of men who couldn't tell a Communist from a liberal, made the early loyalty measures generally ineffective. Inertia and resistance were encouraged by the Communists in government — men whose activities have been succinctly described by the Senate Internal Security Subcommittee:

They hired each other. They promoted each other. They raised each other's salaries. They transferred each other from bureau to bureau, from department to department, from Congressional committee to Congressional committee. They assigned each other to international missions. They *vouched for each other's loyalty and protected each other when exposure threatened.* [Italics added.]

2. Administrative measures

Beginning in 1940 the following administrative measures were taken:

(a) 1940: A Presidential Administrative Order called for FBI investigations when requested by a government agency. (However, of the 1,597 complaints sent on to various departments by the FBI, only 193 resulted in requests for investigation; in 254 cases J. Edgar Hoover was informed that no inquiry was desired; and the other 1,150 were completely ignored by the executive departments.)

(b) 1941: A Presidential Administrative Order authorized the FBI to investigate without a request.

(c) 1942: An interdepartmental committee was set up to act as liaison with the FBI and to advise the departments on how to proceed with FBI complaints. (However, the departments were under no obligation to heed the advice. The result: by 1943, of 4,579 employees against whom complaints had been lodged, 36 had been dismissed and 13 had been transferred to other agencies.)

(d) 1943: A new interdepartmental committee was established by order of President Roosevelt. (But it had little more power than its predecessor. The result: by 1946, 24 persons had been dismissed and 32 others had been disciplined.)

In 1947 President Truman issued Executive Order 9835, which completely overhauled and reorganized the entire loyalty-security program of the Executive Branch. This comprehensive new program at first authorized dismissals when there was "reasonable ground for belief that the person involved is disloyal." Later the criterion of dismissal became "a reasonable doubt of the loyalty of the person involved."

Mr. Truman had good reason to move. The Cold War had begun. And in 1945 top-secret State Department papers had been found in the offices of the pro-Communist magazine *Amerasia*. In 1947 a Communist, Carl Aldo Marzani, was convicted of lying to his State Department superior about his Party membership. A year earlier, a Canadian Royal Commission had corroborated the testimony of Igor Gouzenko, a Soviet code clerk, that a vast Soviet spy network was operating in atomic installations in Canada, Great Britain, and the United States. (The convictions of traitors Allan Nunn May and Klaus Fuchs in England and Harry Gold and the Rosenbergs in the United States resulted from these disclosures.)

Concretely, what was accomplished under the Truman loyalty program?

In June 1953 the Civil Service Loyalty Review Board, set up as the final authority on these matters, reported on its six years of operations. It had considered a total of 26,236 cases (one-half of 1 per cent of the 4,500,000 government employees and applicants). The following dispositions had been made:

In 2,748 cases investigation had been dropped because the persons involved resigned or withdrew their applications.

In 3,634 cases no final decisions had been made for similar reasons.

In 1,015 cases data had been referred to the Army Department, for adjudication under its own more rigorous standards.

Still pending: 1,779 cases.

Total: 9,176 cases.

That left 17,060 cases. In 16,503 of these cases, individuals were adjudged loyal; 557 were dismissed or denied employment — fewer than 2 per cent of all the cases considered by the Loyalty Review Board.

It does not take a trained investigator to see something wrong with this picture: either too many innocent people were being placed in jeopardy, or too many guilty persons were being cleared. Actually, the Truman loyalty program was faulty in both respects. On the one hand, people were jeopardized and even dismissed on trivial grounds, such as reading the *New Republic* or possessing books about Russia. On the other hand, Communists and especially fellow-travelers and Communist-fronters had frequently slipped through the loopholes of the loyalty standards.

Much of the security procedure, of course, was going on behind the scenes. But public equanimity was shattered by the Hiss case — by the sensational charges of Communist infiltration of the State Department sworn to by Whittaker Chambers at public hearings of the House Un-American Activities Committee and at the two trials of Alger Hiss. And the consistent refusal of President Truman and his associates to meet the issue squarely — for instance, their persistence in calling the documented charges a "red herring" — only disturbed the public further.

Whittaker Chambers had testified to Communist subversion as of the late 1930's. But he also intimated that other Communist cells, of which he had no personal knowledge, might still be operating within the government. This was surely enough to set the teeth of Americans on edge.

It is no wonder, then, that a wave of anger, alarm, and dismay swept across the nation when Senator McCarthy stepped onto the stage at Wheeling in 1950[4] — and charged that the State Department was *still* infiltrated by Communists who were helping to shape American foreign policy.

[4] Senator McCarthy, however, did not become overnight the public figure he was by 1954. The early defeats of the Korean War later in 1950 were important in adding to the Senator's following.

That the State Department had been lax, even derelict, in its implementation of the loyalty-security program under President Truman's Executive Order 9835 was evidenced by a significant incident in January 1951. In that month Hiram Bingham, former Republican Senator from Connecticut, became chairman of the Civil Service Loyalty Review Board. One of his first official acts was to convene a special meeting of the board to discuss what to do about an old problem — the State Department security program. Said the chairman:

I think it is fair to say that the State Department, as you know, has the worst record of any department in the action of its Loyalty Board. . . . The Loyalty Board, in all the cases that have been considered in the State Department, has not found anyone — shall I say, "guilty" under our rules. It is the only Board which has acted that way.

At this, another member of the board remarked:

. . . . I don't understand their position at all, because although their board has not held their people ineligible under the loyalty test, who should have been held ineligible under that test — they have plenty of power to remove them as a security risk. Why haven't they exercised it? They haven't exercised it, in spite of all the searchlights that have been turned upon them.

The board's minutes, quoted above, were obtained by Senator McCarthy and turned over to the Senate Appropriations Committee. This was part of the pressure campaign he conducted beginning with his speech of February 9, 1950. After that address in Wheeling, he made another speech in Salt Lake City, sent a telegram to President Truman, and on February 20 addressed the Senate — in each case repeating his charges that the State Department was riddled with Communists who were shaping American foreign policy. As a result of these sensational charges, the Senate appointed a special committee, under the chairmanship of Senator Millard Tydings of Maryland, to investigate "whether persons who are disloyal to the United States are, or have been, employed by the Department of State."

The directive was as simple and clear-cut as that. Yet, instead of following that directive, the Tydings committee attempted chiefly to investigate and discredit McCarthy, principally on the ground of the apparent discrepancies in his series of speeches. Thus most of the hearings were concerned with the numbers and phrases used by the Senator in his Wheeling speech.

Did he say there were 205 Communists in the State Department?

Or was it 57 — or 81? Did he describe them as "card-carrying Communists"? Or did he use the more cautious language of the Senate speech where he quoted himself as having said at Wheeling, "I have in my hand 57 cases of individuals who would appear to be either card-carrying members or certainly loyal to the Communist Party, but who are still helping to shape our foreign policy"?

Actually, the Senator had used all of these figures on different occasions, having prepared them on the basis of several different reports made years earlier by Senate and House groups and by the State Department itself. And indeed the importance of the "numbers game," as McCarthy was later to call it, was exaggerated by his foes for partisan purposes — just as McCarthy himself, by the admission of his strongest supporters, had exaggerated in making his own charges.

But in spite of the exaggerations on both sides McCarthy's essential point was a valid one: the State Department's security program had been lax and frequently ineffective. With this accusation, the Tydings committee, for partisan reasons, lamentably failed to deal.

If the Tydings committee had chosen to discharge its mandate, it could have picked up the broad and trampled trail of Communist infiltration that led from the hastily buried *Amerasia* case to the Institute of Pacific Relations. And if it had picked up this trail, it might well have reached in 1950 the conclusions affirmed by the McCarran committee two years later.

Senator McCarthy presented to the Tydings committee the names of 110 people whom he considered, on the basis of the information he had, to be either loyalty or security risks — or whose presence in the State Department, at one time or another, warranted an investigation of the Department's security procedures. Of these 110 people, 48 were not employed in the Department at the time of the hearings; 62 were so employed — and all of them were cleared in the committee's majority report, which declared that McCarthy's charges were "a fraud and a hoax."

Within a year, however, 49 of the 62 cases cleared by the committee were in security channels. By 1954, at least 18 of McCarthy's "cases" had been separated in one way or another from government service.

Who was on the list? They were a varied group. Among the better-known names were these:

(1) Owen Lattimore, who the McCarran committee later concluded "was from some time in the 1930's a conscious, articulate instrument of the Soviet conspiracy."

(2) William Remington, who was later convicted of perjury in having denied past membership in the Communist Party.

(3) John Stewart Service, who (as mentioned earlier) admitted handing over confidential government documents to the pro-Communist magazine *Amerasia* but nevertheless was cleared by the State Department's Loyalty Security Board on four separate occasions. (Service was finally found by the board to be a security risk and dismissed by the State Department in 1951.)

(4) John Carter Vincent, accused by Louis Budenz in sworn testimony of having once been a member of the Communist Party, later adjudged a loyalty risk by the Civil Service Loyalty Review Board, and finally exonerated by Secretary Dulles, who at the same time requested Vincent's resignation on the ground that he had shown bad judgment.

(5) Oliver E. Clubb, like Service and Vincent a State Department Far East expert, who had fallen under the influence of the Lattimore group, was adjudged a security risk by the Department's Security Board, and resigned immediately after his successful appeal to Secretary Acheson to reverse the ruling.

There were quite a few similar cases; people with bulging records of pro-Communist activities and associations successfully weathered many departmental security hearings, only to be discharged or allowed to resign under fire later — after McCarthy's charges.

Then there was a large group about whom the facts are still ambiguous or indeterminate. Some of them were suspended and discharged, others resigned, still others retained their positions. In many of these cases, the exact facts were impossible to ascertain because the names of the individuals were not widely publicized and the security processes through which they passed were kept confidential.

Also included on McCarthy's list were several persons with well-known and continuing records as fellow-travelers and Communist-fronters, like Frederick Schuman and Harlow Shapley, who — although they were never State Department employees — had served as advisers or consultants at some point prior to McCarthy's public charges.

On the basis of cases such as the foregoing, of which there were many, it was fair to state that the State Department's security procedures were startlingly lax and improper. People like Service and Vincent should never have been cleared once — to say nothing of several times. Apologists for the Soviet Union like Schuman and

Shapley should not have been called on to advise anyone in government on any matter.

In calling public attention to these and similar derelictions, Senator McCarthy and others performed a public service. The subsequent acceleration of the State Department's security processes was certainly the result, at least in part, of the public pressures stimulated by the Senator's activities. This speeding-up process was also the result of the reaction of the whole American people and government to the Communist aggression in Korea.

But there was another facet of Senator McCarthy's early role that gave rise to serious misgivings among many people, including many anti-Communists — liberals and conservatives alike. This was simply the question of the Senator's veracity.

Their skepticism was aroused by his juggling of figures. At one time and another, he had given 205 or 57 or 81 (and he actually presented 110 cases to the Tydings committee) as the number of Communists or pro-Communists in the State Department. He never satisfactorily explained these obvious discrepancies.

Many people were disturbed by the scores of serious misstatements by the Senator in the course of his attacks. William F. Buckley and L. Brent Bozell in their documented defense of the Senator[5] pointed out:

A comparison of the dossier from which McCarthy got his material with McCarthy's own version of this material reveals that in 38 cases he was guilty of exaggeration. On some occasions "fellow-traveller" had turned into "Communist"; on others, "alleged pro-Communist" had developed into "pro-Communist" . . . after McCarthy got through improvising on them, fifteen cases seemed indeed to move up a notch on the security ladder.

Thus McCarthy, instead of presenting Owen Lattimore as the skillful, effective, and influential Party-lining propagandist he was, characterized him as the "top Soviet espionage agent" in America.

Dorothy Kenyon, the first public case dramatically presented by the Senator to the Tydings committee, turned out to be not a member of the Communist Party, but a misguided liberal, who had undoubtedly had some tenuous connections with Communist fronts in the 1930's, but who, beginning with her vigorous denunciation of the Stalin-Hitler pact of 1939, had established an early and overt record of anti-Communism.

[5] *McCarthy and His Enemies* (Chicago: Henry Regnery Company, 1954).

Val Lorwin is another case in point. He figured as one of the Senator's unnamed, numbered cases presented to the Tydings committee — Number 54. Lorwin was subsequently suspended by the State Department, but finally cleared. He thereupon resigned. In 1953 he was indicted for perjury in denying past membership in the Communist Party — the only one of the Senator's 81 cases to be indicted. But in May 1954 the Justice Department dropped its charges against Lorwin, with the admission that there was no evidence to sustain them. It turned out that Lorwin had been a long-time democratic socialist, as he and numerous reputable public figures had all along testified, and that he should never have been included in any list of Communists, or pro-Communists. At the same time, the attorney responsible for the indictment was dismissed by the Justice Department.

The Senator's implicit charge of treason against General George Marshall also disturbed large segments of the American people, who knew the general to be a man of integrity and stature, a military leader of unquestionable loyalty.

Furthermore, the Senator never presented any evidence of past or present membership in the Communist Party on the part of any of the persons he named in any of his lists.

These and many other examples of exaggeration and distortion of charges and evidence were excused by many defenders of Senator McCarthy on the ground that the attention he aroused and the investigations he instigated (such as the sober and devastatingly factual hearings conducted by the McCarran committee) were valuable contributions to public education and to the tightening of government security procedures. The Senator's defenders also pointed to the indubitable fact that McCarthy was opposed by a partisan and antagonistic Congress and Executive. They claimed that he conducted his campaign virtually singlehanded and against great odds, enjoying no authority or powerful position in the Senate and lacking any means except publicity for obtaining the facts, exerting pressure, and arousing the public.

With the Republican victory in the 1952 election, the Senator's defenders — and indeed many of his enemies — predicted that he would change his course and his tactics; with a Republican Congress and a friendly Republican President, McCarthy would no longer need to exaggerate and distort. In a newly won position of power and authority, the Senator could be expected to increase his sense of responsibility and his accuracy.

McCarthy himself encouraged this expectation when in November 1952, a few days after President Eisenhower's election, he publicly acknowledged the implications of his changed position. In answer to an inquiry by Frederick Woltman, Pulitzer Prize-winning Scripps-Howard reporter, the Senator declared that the Eighty-third Congress would see a "new McCarthy," since it would no longer be necessary for him to conduct a one-man campaign to expose Communists in government. "We have a new President," said the Senator, "and he will conduct the fight."

That was at the end of 1952. Since then, the nation has been able to witness the activities of Senator McCarthy as chairman of the Senate Permanent Subcommittee on Investigations. How has he discharged his new responsibilities? In what way has he lived up to the expectations of his friends, the fears of his enemies, and his own forthright promises?

2. Senator McCarthy at Work

"Every man takes the limits of his own field of vision for the limits of the world."

SCHOPENHAUER, *Psychological Observations*

"One must have a good memory to be able to keep the promises one makes."

NIETZSCHE, *Human, All Too Human*

Prologue: The Case for Senator McCarthy

This book is not a biography of Senator McCarthy. It is, as the title indicates, an analysis of the Senator's role in the fight against Communist infiltration of the United States government.

More specifically, it is a case study of McCarthy in power and of the part his anti-Communism has played in his public career since his assumption in January 1953 of the chairmanship of the Senate Permanent Subcommittee on Investigations.

What is the case for Senator McCarthy? His public role as an anti-Communist campaigner has had two aspects: (a) that of scourge; and (b) that of public educator.

What has been his record of achievement in these two fields? As scourge, he has tried to root out of the government any Communists or pro-Communists who might be discovered there. As public educator, he has tried to make people more aware of the dangers of Communist infiltration. There is no doubt that Senator McCarthy has called attention to dubious practices in the government's handling of pro-Communist infiltration into government agencies. Although he was not the first anti-Communist campaigner to call public attention to lax security procedures in the State Department, he alerted many people who had not previously been aware of the problem to the danger of Communist infiltration and to the fact that this infiltration had not been handled promptly and effectively by a number of government agencies even when the facts were available to them. The subsequent tightening of government security procedures stemmed, at least in part, from the

16

Senator's charges in public forums and during the Tydings committee hearings. So also did the establishment of the McCarran committee, which later investigated the nature and extent of Communist infiltration into government, education, and communications media. Some of the persons named by Senator McCarthy as security risks resigned or were dismissed from their positions.

What of Senator McCarthy's role after 1953? During the summer of 1953 the McCarthy subcommittee turned up an employee of the Government Printing Office — a Legislative, not an Executive agency, supervised by a joint Congressional committee under the chairmanship of Senator William Jenner — who had access to classified information and who pleaded the protection of the Fifth Amendment in the face of charges of Communist affiliations. A number of government agencies, including the information program, the Government Printing Office, and the Army, reassessed aspects of their programs and procedures under the spotlight of investigation or threatened investigation.

There is no doubt that the furor aroused by Senator McCarthy in several instances caused many persons to reconsider problems about Communism that they had tended to ignore.

Should there be books by Communist authors on the shelves of government libraries abroad?

Should the United States ignore the trade of its allies with Soviet satellites in Europe and with Communist China at a time when the nation was, in a sense, at war with Communism?

Should Communists continue to receive commissions and honorable discharges from the United States Army? (After the uproar over the "pink dentist," Major Peress, the Army changed its rules so that all persons found to be security risks, if discovered by the Army, would be immediately discharged "under other than honorable conditions.")

Should persons who plead the protection of the Fifth Amendment during Congressional investigations of private industries holding government defense contracts be allowed to remain in the employ of those industries? (The General Electric Company, after a McCarthy investigation, adopted the policy that any such employee would be dismissed.)

To these questions, Senator McCarthy said: "No." And many Americans agreed with him.

Senator McCarthy has stated that his activities are based on the assumption that, as long as the international Communist conspiracy, sparked by Kremlin directives, continues to function, there remains the danger of Communist infiltration and subversion of the United States government and American institutions. It is his assumption that it is the duty of legislative, executive, and private groups to uncover and prevent such infiltration. With this assumption we are in full agreement. The purpose of this analysis of Senator McCarthy in power is to compare the criteria necessary for an effective anti-Communist campaign with the activities of Senator McCarthy — to apply the plumb-line of fact to determine how the Senator has measured up to these principles.

There are three criteria which must be applied in judging the sincerity and effectiveness of an anti-Communist campaign. Such a campaign must:

1. Identify the enemy clearly

The enemy is Communism. Its ranks comprise Communists, pro-Communists, fellow-travelers, spies, and Communist agents. Its works include infiltration, subversion, and espionage in government and in all other areas of public life.

2. Pinpoint the enemy unmistakably

The target is Communism. It must not be confused with liberalism, socialism, or any other democratic philosophy and program. One must hit the target with the hard facts on infiltration, subversion, or espionage.

3. Expose the enemy persistently and relentlessly

The objective is to eliminate Communism from any role it may have in the conduct of our public affairs. One must never stop hammering the facts home. One must pursue the enemy until he is driven out.

How does Senator McCarthy measure up to these criteria?

We think the simplest and fairest way of answering the question is to examine his record as chairman of the Senate Permanent Subcommittee on Investigations. In this position of power, authority, and responsibility, the Senator has been able to write his own ticket. What have been his achievements?

The pattern and record established by Senator McCarthy rest primarily on two major investigations he conducted as chairman of the Senate subcommittee: the State Department's International Information Administration (including the Voice of America), and the Army's Signal Center at Fort Monmouth, New Jersey. An analysis of these two investigations and a survey of his other activities since January 1953 ought to show how the Senator measures up to the three standards of an anti-Communist crusade.

I. THE INTERNATIONAL INFORMATION ADMINISTRATION

The International Information Administration came into being as an agency of the State Department under the authority of Public Law 402, passed by the Eightieth Congress on January 27, 1948. Under the terms of this law, the information service was to be a means of disseminating abroad information about the United States and its foreign policies; it had as its larger objective the promotion of better understanding between the American people and other nations. It rapidly became a major instrument of America's Cold War strategy.

Despite this role, the program always operated under a number of serious handicaps. To begin with, the idea of a propaganda agency was quite foreign to the American people. The very word "propaganda" carried traditional connotations unpleasing to the American ear. And the function and work of this agency were not particularly well known or understood by the public.

There were a few distinguished men of vision who grasped the potential of an effort to pierce the Iron Curtain with a message of freedom and truth and to encourage understanding of America in the free world. But these men made their inquiries and recommendations quietly and on the whole ineffectively, as "advisory commissions," "psychological warfare boards," and the like — largely unheeded by the people, the Congress, or the Executive.

Nor did the information service meet with much sympathy in its home territory, the State Department. The men of State, unaccustomed to this type of work, were in general rather uneasy about their relationship with the new agency. In addition, State viewed the International Information Administration with a jaundiced eye for bringing into the Department many old employees of the Office of War Information (OWI), a transfer which the diplomats later had good cause to rue. According to a 1950 State Department memorandum, there were hundreds of OWI employees, transferred into the Department in 1947, who had never been fully investigated. Some of them, although by no means the majority, had dubious political records, and this situation exacerbated the Department's already complicated security problem.

Economy-minded Congressmen, of whom there was no dearth in the Eightieth and subsequent Congresses, were equally suspicious of this strange, new, expensive agency which they themselves had spawned in what now appeared to them to have been a thoughtless, incautious moment. The information agency, like all other government departments, had to face a querulous Congress once a year, at appropriation season — and, unlike other government departments, it had to justify not merely its specific projects but its very existence.

All these factors were not conducive to a feeling of stability and continuity in the program. Nevertheless the agency went along doing its work, subject to countless reorganizations and much advice, more or less in the shadow of public affairs. It gained the plaudits of many escapees from behind the Iron Curtain, who testified to its effectiveness in broadcasting the truth and in keeping alive hopes of liberation in the hearts of Soviet-dominated peoples. It even got a backhanded compliment from the Kremlin — which annually spent $1,000,000,000 (ten times the U. S. information agency's annual budget) merely to jam the Voice of America.

When the information program finally came to public attention, it hit the front page. The American public, the Congress, the Executive, and the whole world were apprised by Senator McCarthy that it was less the Voice of America than the "Voice of Moscow."[1]

How did Senator McCarthy in this investigation measure up to the criteria of an effective anti-Communist crusade?

1. *Identify the enemy clearly*
2. *Pinpoint the enemy unmistakably*
3. *Expose the enemy persistently and relentlessly*

Quite early in the proceedings, the Senator clearly identified the enemy. He charged that the anti-Communist information program had been deliberately subverted by Communist infiltration and sabotage.

---

[1] Voice of America hearings, p. 185. The printed record of this investigation is as follows. There were two sets of hearings: (a) on the Voice of America itself, comprising 775 pages of testimony and exhibits; and (b) on the overseas information centers, comprising 496 pages. In addition, the subcommittee filed three reports to the Senate: two interim reports, entitled "Waste and Mismanagement in Voice of America Engineering Projects" and "United States Information Service," both filed January 25, 1954; and a final report, entitled "Voice of America," filed February 3, 1954.

How unmistakably did the Senator pinpoint the enemy? How many Communists, pro-Communists, and fellow-travelers did he uncover? What evidence did he present of infiltration and sabotage?

How thoroughly did he expose and pursue the enemy? How many Communists and pro-Communists did he rout? How did he carry through on his own charges?

Senator McCarthy investigated six major areas of the information program: (A) the French Desk of the Voice of America; (B) Latin-American broadcasts of the Voice of America; (C) engineering projects of the Voice of America; (D) the office of the Voice of America's policy adviser; (E) the Deputy Administrator of the International Information Administration; and (F) the overseas libraries. Let us examine Senator McCarthy's achievements in each of these areas of investigation.

A. The French Desk of the Voice of America

The charges against the very important French Desk (the section of the Voice that broadcasts to France) added up to an allegation of anti-American programming and — by extension — of pro-Communist broadcasting. These charges were made during the hearings, and some of them were briefly referred to in the McCarthy committee report on the Voice of America.[2] This is how Senator McCarthy himself summed them up at one point in the hearings:

CHAIRMAN. Let me ask you this: If I were a member of the Communist Party, and I wanted to discredit America and further the Communist cause, could you think of any better job I could do helping out the Communist cause than by beaming to Europe the type of material which you have just described?

MR. HORNEFFER. No, sir; not possibly.

CHAIRMAN. In other words, you feel we are doing a great service to the Communist cause in beaming this material out in the so-called fight against Communism.

A perusal of the handling of the specific charges in this case raises some interesting points:

(1) The acting chief of the French Desk, Troup Mathews, had allegedly invited a new employee, Nancy Lenkeith, to join a "collectivist, Marxist colony" he was proposing to set up.

This charge was made at a public hearing. But Mathews was never called to a public session to affirm or deny the charge.

---

[2] All three reports on the information program were reportedly written by G. David Schine, who figured so prominently in the Army-McCarthy hearings. See Appendix B below.

(2) The chief of the Desk, Fernand Auberjonois, allegedly had called Whittaker Chambers a psychopath and ordered that Chambers' book *Witness* not be used as source material for scripts.

But Auberjonois testified he could not recall having made such remarks. He conceded that he opposed using the Chambers book; but he was given no opportunity to explain his reasons. He was cut off at just that point.

(3) Miss Lenkeith claimed she was fired because she was an anti-Communist, as evidenced — she said — by her insistence on reviewing the Chambers book.

But the book was reviewed with the approval of Walter Ducloux, Desk chief at the time.

(4) Miss Lenkeith alleged that the policy adviser of the Voice, Edwin Kretzmann, had indicated opposition to the review of the Chambers book.

Kretzmann testified, but he was not questioned about this allegation.

(5) Miss Lenkeith testified that she had been fired at a meeting attended by Ducloux and by the deputy chief of operations for the Voice, Dwight Herrick.

But neither Ducloux nor Herrick was called to testify on this point.

(6) The chief of operations of the Voice, Alfred Puhan, had allegedly called Marcelle Henry, a member of the Desk, "subversive."

Puhan testified, but he was not questioned about this allegation.

(7) Miss Henry had allegedly written scripts criticizing conditions in the state of Texas, indirectly favoring the ideas of Karl Marx, and referring to "those dirty Americans."

But she was never called to a public session to testify on the matter.

(8) The Desk allegedly broadcast scripts attacking Wall Street, belittling American culture, and presenting a picture of a dissolute, degenerate America.

None of the full scripts allegedly containing this material was entered into the record as evidence. And no representative of the Desk was asked at a public hearing to comment on the charges.

(9) The Desk allegedly broadcast, without comment or rebuttal and by the directive of both the Desk chief and the Voice's policy adviser, a complete speech by Jakob Malik, Soviet delegate to the United Nations.

Neither the Desk chief nor the policy adviser was asked during his testimony to comment on this charge.

(10) Instead of being asked about all these weighty charges, the Desk chief, Auberjonois, was examined closely concerning a script prepared by an outside private organization. That organization was headed by a man named as a Communist, and the script purportedly included a short interview with Charlie Chaplin, who has a fellow-traveling political record.

The script, however, dealt not with Chaplin's political views, but with highlights of Hollywood. It was prepared in response to considerable overseas interest in the United States movie-production center. And the script was never used.

Here was a series of sensational charges adding up to accusations of Communist infiltration and of sabotage of anti-Communist programming. The charges were made, names were named, in public, televised hearings.

But none of the charges was corroborated. No evidence was introduced to substantiate them. No Communists, pro-Communists, or fellow-travelers were named or exposed. And all the apparent leads to a pro-Communist cell were never followed up.

How are we to account for Senator McCarthy's failure to pinpoint or expose any element of infiltration or subversion? We must conclude either that he never seriously entertained these charges, or that he was not really interested in following them up, once they had been aired.

B. Latin-American Broadcasts of the Voice of America

A substantial portion of the Voice of America hearings was devoted to the investigation of charges of pro-Communism in script material used for Latin America. The charges covered 30 pages of transcript.

The charges were refuted by a mass of documentary evidence. This evidence was filed — but never made part of the record.

The rebuttals by three of the people accused of pro-Communist bias comprised 38 pages of transcript. It is clear that they were afforded ample opportunity to deny aspersions on their loyalty.

But there was this difference: The charges were televised. The rebuttals, though in public session, were not televised.

Why did Senator McCarthy allow the charges to be aired in the first place, since they could be refuted by documentary evidence?

Why were the charges — but not the rebuttals — televised?

In this case — obviously a minor one — the Senator's purpose seemed to be chiefly to set the television stage for further sensational allegations.

Here again the charges were wide of the mark. No Communists were named, exposed, or routed. The standards for an effective anti-Communist campaign were not met.

C.   Engineering Projects of the Voice of America

In the course of many days of testimony, Senator McCarthy repeatedly alleged or implied the existence of a pattern of deliberate pro-Communist sabotage in Voice of America engineering projects for building U.S.-based transmitters. These were the charges:

(1) Technical testimony to the effect that two huge transmitting stations, to be constructed on the East and West Coasts of the United States at a cost of $9,000,000 each, were mislocated.

(2) The claim that this mislocation constituted waste and mismanagement.

(3) The allegation that such waste must have been the result not of incompetence but of deliberate sabotage.

Senator McCarthy repeatedly summed up these charges in such terms as the following:

THE CHAIRMAN. Let us put it this way: Let us assume we have a good Voice of America, a voice that is really the Voice of America. Assume I do not want that to reach Communist territory. Would not the best way to sabotage that voice be to place your transmitters within that magnetic storm area, so that you would have this tremendous interference?

THE CHAIRMAN. Now, has it ever been suggested by those who have worked with you in the Voice that this mislocation of stations, the waste in the construction program, has not been entirely as a result of incompetence, but that some of it may have been purposely planned that way?

THE CHAIRMAN. Let me ask you this: If I were in your Department, and I were a member of the Communist Party attempting to sabotage the Voice Program, would it not be wise for me to try and locate the stations within that magnetic storm area so they would be subject to jamming by Communist Russia and so that we could not hit the target area with radio signals? . . . Do you think that mislocation of those two stations was the result of stupidity or the result of a deliberate attempt to sabotage the Voice?

How did Senator McCarthy in this instance measure up to the criteria for an effective anti-Communist crusade?

No fact or evidence of any kind was submitted to substantiate the charge of sabotage. No Communists or fellow-travelers were named, exposed, or routed.

Even the charge of waste was not definitively established. Much evidence and testimony to the effect that the transmitters were not mislocated — information volunteered both during and after the hearings — was ignored.

Could Senator McCarthy have been serious when he leveled the charge before the television cameras? If he had been serious, would he not have fulfilled the requirements for an effective anti-Communist drive, rather than leaving these sensational charges unsubstantiated?

D. The Office of the Voice of America's Policy Adviser

This section of the hearings approached more closely the heart of the investigation — the policy-making mechanism of the International Information Administration. Policy was actually made at the Washington headquarters. The New York headquarters of the Voice of America — the radio branch of the information agency — had a policy adviser to transmit and interpret Washington policy.

A number of serious charges alleging pro-Communism having been leveled at the policy adviser, Edwin Kretzmann, Senator McCarthy interrogated him about some of them. The subcommittee had not summoned Kretzmann; he had voluntarily hurried down to Washington "to clear up some misunderstandings" that had arisen in testimony earlier the same day.

Though Senator McCarthy indicated that he was not prepared then to ask Kretzmann the many questions he had in mind, he promised that "we have a good deal to interrogate you on later." (The Senator did not follow through, and Kretzmann was not asked to appear again.) The Senator took the opportunity to question him anyway on the following points:

(1) The first concerned alleged atheist influence on the Voice. A witness testified that Kretzmann had informed him of having told a third person that the director of religious programming, Roger Lyons, was an atheist.

Kretzmann explained that this was a misunderstanding. A superior had once inquired about Lyons' specific sectarian adherence, and Kretzmann had replied that this was not a pertinent question to ask. And he had added laughingly, "For all I know, he may be an atheist." Kretzmann testified that he knew, on the basis of a thorough discussion with Lyons, that he was a man of profound religious beliefs.

Lyons himself testified categorically that he was not an atheist, that he believed in God, and that he had been a student of religion for many years under Paul Tillich, world-famous Protestant theologian, and Karl Jung, celebrated psychologist.

Nevertheless, the final report on the Voice of America made a point of the fact that "Kretzmann did not consider it pertinent to inquire of the head of the religious desk whether he was an atheist."

Since Senator McCarthy seemed so concerned about the problem, a consistent anti-Communist interest should have led him to pursue the matter by investigating the content of the scripts produced under the religious program to determine whether an alleged atheist had given Voice scripts a pro-Communist bias.

Senator McCarthy did not do this.

Furthermore, though Lyons had testified that it was Alfred Puhan, chief of operations, who had appointed him and was his immediate superior, Senator McCarthy never questioned Puhan on this.

Thus a sensational charge was aired and never persistently followed through. Here was another instance where the target was missed — and no Communist found or exposed.

(2) Senator McCarthy accused Kretzmann of following the *Daily Worker* line in attacking Korean President Syngman Rhee. The Senator cited one script that had provoked the Korean government to revoke the facilities it had previously made available to the Voice of America.

Kretzmann pointed out that he himself, while ultimately responsible, had been away from his office that day; that it was his deputy, Gordon Knox, who had approved the script; that the approval was based on Knox's misunderstanding of a directive from Bradley Connors, policy chief for the International Information Administration.

Neither Connors nor Knox was ever questioned on this critical matter.

Kretzmann, indicating his own disapproval of the script, offered to spread on the record hundreds of pro-Rhee, pro-South Korea scripts.

This offer was never accepted.

On the contrary, in the final report Kretzmann was accused of "the incredible act" of conducting an anti-South Korea campaign.

If the Senator was not satisfied with Kretzmann's testimony and offer, why did he not attempt to substantiate his charge?

Here was another charge that was never explored, an allegation not followed through.

(3) A witness had testified that Kretzmann's office had turned down a strongly anti-Communist script.

Again, it was Knox who had rejected it. But he was never called to explain his action.

Why not? Could it have been because his annotations of the script clearly indicated that his objections to it were based not on its anti-Communist character but on what he took to be its faulty reasoning and its literary weakness?

In this event, Senator McCarthy could not have been serious in entertaining the charge. And a spurious charge has no place in an effective anti-Communist fight.

(4) McCarthy questioned Kretzmann closely about Bertram D. Wolfe, an ex-Communist who was at that time chief of the ideological advisory unit of the Voice of America. The Senator echoed deep suspicions that had been raised about Wolfe by Rep. Fred E. Busbey (Ill.), who under Congressional immunity had falsely accused Wolfe of being a Communist. Wolfe was never called to the witness stand. His voluminous writings for at least a 15-year period prior to 1953 were not examined; a study of them would have indicated his unmistakable anti-Communism.

Here was another charge that could not have been taken seriously by Senator McCarthy. Why would a serious anti-Communist air frivolous charges?

(5) As indicated earlier, Kretzmann was never interrogated about his alleged opposition to the use of Whittaker Chambers' book by the French Desk, nor about his alleged directive ordering that Desk to broadcast an unrebutted speech by Jakob Malik. Why no questions?

(6) Kretzmann was never queried about the grave charge brought against him that he believed the Voice of America was not in the business of fighting Communism. Why no questions?

(7) It had been charged that Fernand Auberjonois, former chief of the French Desk, had been removed from that position because of certain accusations, and had been promoted to a position on the Voice of America's policy staff.

Neither Kretzmann nor Auberjonois was questioned about this seemingly unwise move. Why not?

Here was a long series of grave charges pointing to an allegedly suspicious set-up at the policy-making heart of the Voice of America. How did Senator McCarthy in this instance measure up to the criteria for effective anti-Communism?

He leveled charges that he himself did not take seriously enough to pursue. No evidence was presented to back up any charge. No Communist, fellow-traveler, or dupe was exposed and driven from office. None of the widely publicized accusations was probed beyond its television value. No interest was shown in pursuing presumed leads. The criteria for effective anti-Communism were ignored.

E.   The Deputy Administrator of the International Information Administration

The climax of the investigation was reached in the interrogation of Reed Harris, deputy administrator of the International Information Administration. He figured, directly and indirectly, in nearly one-third of the testimony on the Voice of America. It was clear from the nature of the questioning to which he was subjected that Senator McCarthy considered him the focal point of the sensational charges and implications of a pro-Communist conspiracy in the International Information Administration. The charges against Harris involved, first, allegedly deliberate sabotage of anti-Communist Hebrew programming to Israel; and, second, his youthful affiliations and associations of a pro-Communist nature.

1.   Alleged sabotage of anti-Communist Hebrew programming

In July 1952 the information agency issued a memorandum ordering various cuts in Voice of America programming, based on an economy drive necessitated by decreased Congressional appropriations. The Hebrew Desk was included in the cuts. Voice officials in New York protested against the order, and it remained the subject of inter-office debate and memoranda.

In November 1952 anti-Semitic purges began in the Soviet satellites; later they spread to the Soviet Union itself. The chief of the Hebrew Desk and his superior, the chief of the Near Eastern Division, then protested against the cut on the ground that it would eliminate an effective anti-Communist weapon at a time when maximum advantage could be taken of Soviet-bloc anti-Semitism. They aired the same complaint before the McCarthy subcommittee.

Officials of the International Information Administration insisted that budgetary requirements had necessitated the cut. Because the orders had been signed by Reed Harris, the charges of "sabotage" centered on him.

This is how Senator McCarthy stated the charge, on only one of several occasions:

CHAIRMAN. And am I correct in this, that you feel that the reason why the Hebrew language desk was being discontinued was because it was doing a good job of combatting communism?

MR. DOOHER [Chief of the Near Eastern Division]. Again, sir, I don't want to go into the thinking of the people who gave the directive, but the result was the same.

CHAIRMAN. Let us put it this way: If I had been in a position of power, if I were an ardent member of the Communist Party, would I not have taken the same action that was taken to discontinue the Hebrew language desk, at a time when Communist Russia became openly anti-Semitic, at a time when we had this great counter-propaganda weapon?

MR. DOOHER. I believe so, sir.

CHAIRMAN. So that while you do not want to delve into the minds of individuals —

MR. DOOHER. No, sir.

CHAIRMAN. And you do not propose to examine their motives, you feel that the action would have been the same had they been representing Joe Stalin?

MR. DOOHER. That is correct, sir. . . .

CHAIRMAN. And as far as you are concerned, when you put a gun to a man's head and pull the trigger, if there is a bullet in the gun, he is just as dead whether you intended to kill him or not.

Here was a dramatic instance of the charge of pro-Communist sabotage. How effectively did Senator McCarthy in this instance wage his anti-Communist campaign?

No evidence, documentary or circumstantial, was introduced to substantiate the allegation. Reed Harris took full responsibility for ordering the cut, but no facts were adduced to indicate any pro-Communist motives on his part. No attempt was carried through, beyond the expression and elicitation of opinion, to connect him with any Communist plan or with a conspiracy to stifle anti-Communist programming.

2. Harris' youthful pro-Communist associations

Senator McCarthy relied on assertions of youthful pro-Communist associations to establish the allegation of Harris' pro-Communist bias. These were the major components of the charge:

(a) Twenty-one years earlier, in 1932, Harris had written a book, *King Football,* dealing mostly with the evils of commercialized college sports. In this book, written when he was a student at Columbia University, Harris incidentally expressed the view that a teacher ought to have the academic right to expound Communism if he believed in it. He also urged that Communists should not be deprived of the opportunity to hold teaching positions.

At the McCarthy hearing, Harris testified that he had long since repudiated the views of what he himself called a "sophomoric" book. He pointed out, however, that Senator Taft in 1953 espoused the view that Communists should be allowed to teach — a position Harris himself had rejected long before.

(b) Harris had been suspended from Columbia for certain opinions he had expressed as editor of the student paper. He was later reinstated. Senator McCarthy charged that in his fight for reinstatement he was provided with a lawyer by the American Civil Liberties Union, "cited as a Communist-front organization."

The ACLU was never a Communist front, and was never cited as such either by the Attorney General or by the House Committee on Un-American Activities.[3] McCarthy also did not mention that *just a few weeks before he leveled this charge,* the chief counsel of his own subcommittee, Roy Cohn, had addressed an ACLU forum.

(c) Senator McCarthy charged Harris with membership in a number of Communist-front organizations, such as the American Students Union and the League of American Writers.

At the hearings Harris testified that he could not remember the precise details of these alleged memberships or sponsorships, dating back a dozen and more years. But he recalled that in each case his association had been very brief. And in a subsequent letter to the Senator he offered documentary proof that he had briefly shared these associations with such stalwart anti-Communists as Senator Paul Douglas and author Louis Bromfield — and that he had left as soon as he detected a Communist take-over.

Despite this evidence, McCarthy's final report reverted to these associations as indicative of Harris' pro-Communism. But the Senator gave no indication of having probed the matter further and of having come up with conclusive evidence of pro-Communist leanings on Harris' part.

---

[3] It had been falsely cited in the notoriously inaccurate 1943 report of the California Un-American Activities Committee, headed by State Senator Jack B. Tenney.

How well did Senator McCarthy in the Harris case measure up to the standards for an effective anti-Communist crusade?

He offered no evidence that Harris was or had ever been a Communist, a pro-Communist, or a fellow-traveler. Senator McCarthy failed to connect Harris with a Communist conspiracy to commit sabotage. In the attack on Harris, no Communist enemy was pinpointed, no Communist influence exposed and eliminated. And, having aired the sensational charges on television, the Senator lost all further interest in them.

F. The Overseas Libraries

Senator McCarthy charged that the information program's overseas libraries were flooded with Communist books — some 30,000 of them. His allegations and the testimony elicited during the hearings (which were separate from the Voice of America hearings) gave the impression of wholesale subversion of the information program.

In establishing a policy for its overseas libraries the State Department took its lead from a specially created advisory commission, which included the presidents of Princeton, Wisconsin, Minnesota, and Catholic Universities. The criterion they had unanimously recommended was this: "The content of the book, regardless of authorship, [should] be the criterion which determines its availability for inclusion in USIS [United States Information Service] libraries."

This recommendation was embodied in an International Information Administration policy directive, dated February 3, 1953. The directive also permitted the use, in special cases, of Communist or controversial authors, if it could be clearly established that such use was, on balance, beneficial to our propaganda aims.

What was the idea behind this policy? Essentially it had a long-range psychological-warfare objective: to impress the foreign public with the fact that the United States government libraries abroad were just as free as American libraries at home — truly representative of our free way of life. Thus the overseas libraries would display literature reflecting the widest range of views. The purpose was to avoid making these libraries look like another out-and-out propaganda agency, expressing only an accepted, official viewpoint. And they would serve also as a vivid contrast to the Soviet information centers, whose one-sided propagandistic tone, quality, and content were so obvious that they were universally mocked and discredited in the very countries they sought to influence. Thus, for example, the State Department, under a Democratic administration, distributed thousands of copies of such magazines as *Life, Time, Collier's, Reader's Digest* — all of which at times showed clear antagonism to the Democratic administration.

Such a policy, it was argued, would be a striking example of democracy in action, would lend credibility to any message the United States might seek to get across, and would generally enhance the prestige of this country in the minds of critical foreigners.

This was, of course, only one side of the case. The opposing viewpoint was quite simple: Such a policy countenances the purchase, use, and display of Communist literature. This very fact means that such literature bears the stamp of approval of the United States government. It is misleading to the foreign public, and it is a waste of taxpayers' money. On general principles there should be no room in government libraries overseas for any Communist or pro-Communist literature, the argument ran.

In addition, there were certain special problems relating to the overseas libraries. Most of the books in these libraries had been acquired as gifts or free acquisitions during the war, the period of the Grand Alliance against the Nazis. No directive had ever been put out to revise these wartime booklists — among other reasons, because it would have been an extremely expensive job to cut all of them. However, most of the overseas librarians had themselves done a judicious pruning job during the post-war years, and their lists were, by all accounts, generally satisfactory.

The situation was different in Germany. Observers such as writer Norbert Muhlen reported on a number of occasions that there were not nearly as many anti-Communist books on the library shelves of U. S. information centers in Germany as there might have been. Although there was a wide and varied selection of acceptable magazines available, the display of magazines was lopsided. The *Nation,* for example, whose content for a long period betrayed a susceptibility to Communist apologetics, was prominently displayed, while the *New Leader,* a staunch anti-Communist periodical of long standing, was not readily accessible.

Germany, however, was not typical, as can readily be understood. There, the library projects, as part of the larger information program, had from the beginning had one, single-minded objective, established by the highest Allied policy: anti-Nazism and democratization. The over-all Allied policy gradually shifted in the post-war years from a wholly anti-Nazi policy to major emphasis on the strengthening of the free West German Republic as part of the Western coalition in the Cold War. But there was a time lag, induced largely by bureaucratic and budgetary factors, during which the library program slowly caught up with the changed over-all policy.

This debate had been going on for several years before Mc-Carthy entered the picture. When he did get into it, he transformed the terms of the debate by charging wholesale subversion of the overseas library program.

The Senator had clearly identified the enemy. How unmistakably did he pinpoint infiltration and subversion in the libraries? How persistent and relentless was he in pursuing the enemy?

The parade of well-known Communists

Senator McCarthy sought to dramatize his charge by interrogating a series of well-known Communists, some of whose books were found to have been on the shelves of overseas libraries. Fully one-half of the testimony in this hearing was given over to the largely uncommunicative testimony of these authors. Most of the time was spent wrangling with them about their refusal to answer questions as to whether or not they were Communists.

What purpose was served by sandwiching these individuals in with government witnesses?

They had no role in determining the over-all policy for the overseas libraries. They had no contact with the men who did, and Senator McCarthy did not try to prove the existence of such contact. They were not consulted when their books were chosen and purchased for display on the library shelves. They were unaware of the presence of their books on the shelves, and Senator McCarthy did not claim they had anything to do with it.

The appearance of these Communist writers under the television lights seemed irrelevant to the objective of striking at Communist infiltration in overseas libraries.

The policy debate

Senator McCarthy made it clear that he opposed the presence of Communist literature on the library shelves. He considered this simply infiltration and subversion.

But he gave no indication that there might be another side to the question, that this might be a question of calculated policy. For example, he called no one to testify in any terms comparable to those used by Under-Secretary of State Walter Bedell Smith, testifying at a later date and to another Senate committee: "I can say categorically that the Secretary of State is and has been opposed to the works of Communist authors *per se*. . . . But the overseas libraries must be free to put Communist works on their shelves if they can be used to counter Soviet propaganda."

Does General Smith's testimony add up to a subversive plot? If so, an effective and persistent anti-Communist investigator would have called upon General Smith to explain himself and would have tried to get this "infiltrator" out of office. Senator McCarthy did not pursue this line.

And, if this were a subversive plot, an effective anti-Communist would have sought to question the men whose recommendations were the basis for this policy — the presidents of Minnesota, Wisconsin, Princeton, and Catholic Universities. Senator McCarthy failed to look into their backgrounds and motives. Had he done so, he might perhaps have discovered that the basis of the policy was not pro-Communist, but skillfully anti-Communist.

The Wechsler case

A prime example of Communist infiltration, according to Senator McCarthy, was the alleged presence on overseas library shelves of books by James Wechsler, editor of the New York *Post*. McCarthy cited the fact that Wechsler had once been a member of the Young Communist League. The Senator evidently considered Wechsler's case of extreme importance, for his testimony occupied more space than that of any other individual in these hearings.

Measured against the criteria of pinpointing and exposing the enemy, this case was far wide of the mark. Wechsler had indeed once been a member of the Young Communist League — but this fact was a matter of public and FBI knowledge. Wechsler had himself made it public, and he had co-operated with the FBI.

It was also public knowledge that Wechsler had, since 1937 (thirteen years before Senator McCarthy appeared on the anti-Communist front), made a demonstrable record of fighting Communism in his work and writing.

He helped defeat the Communist effort to take over the Newspaper Guild in the late 1930's.

He resigned from the newspaper *PM* when he felt it had been infiltrated beyond his power to combat Communist influence.

He wrote a book (1940) on John L. Lewis, a chapter of which

demonstrated the insidious manner in which Communists attempted to infiltrate labor unions.

He had been against the Nazi-Soviet pact in 1939. And in 1948 he took a vigorous public stand endorsing the credibility and historical significance of Whittaker Chambers' testimony.

He read to the Senator a 1952 Communist Party resolution attacking himself. McCarthy's only response was: "Did you have anything to do with the passage of that resolution?"

What anti-Communist purpose was served by harassing Wechsler, an anti-Communist liberal? Senator McCarthy hardly mentioned Wechsler's books — so that Wechsler never learned which of his books had been the ostensible reason for his being called before the subcommittee.

In this part of Senator McCarthy's investigation no pro-Communist book was mentioned. No proven Communist was named or turned out of government office. This effort to confuse a liberal with a Communist contradicts all the criteria of an effective anti-Communist campaign.

The case of Theodore Kaghan

In April 1953 Theodore Kaghan finally made his long-heralded appearance before the McCarthy committee. Two months before, at the Voice of America hearings, he had been publicly branded a "pseudo-American." It had been charged that he had continued to work for the State Department's information program despite his alleged failure to get security clearance. Senator McCarthy obviously considered this case another prime example of Communist infiltration: Kaghan's testimony occupied almost as much time as that of James Wechsler.

Who was Theodore Kaghan? He was acting deputy director of the Public Affairs Division of the High Commissioner's office in Germany. In that capacity he was the Number Two Man in America's information program in Germany. If Theodore Kaghan were really a Communist infiltrator and subversive, the matter would be serious indeed.

He was never accused of being a member of the Communist Party. He was accused of having shared his apartment with a Communist in 1939. He readily admitted that he had assumed his roommate was a Communist.

He was accused of having signed a petition to get a Communist Party candidate on the ballot in a 1939 New York City Council election. Again he unhesitatingly agreed that he had done this. His reason: At the time he felt that every party ought to have a chance to place its candidate before the public.

He was accused of having continued his intermittent associations with Communists and their sympathizers during the period of the Hitler-Stalin pact. Kaghan agreed that some of his associations in those years could well have been with Communists. He did not excuse himself; he frankly admitted that he was simply not as politically aware at that time as he subsequently became. Communism, although it did not appeal to him as a doctrine, appeared to him at that time to be just another political party, distasteful perhaps, but not abhorrent. He learned better, he maintained, during World War II.

Finally, he was accused of having written pro-Communist plays during his college days. McCarthy read sample passages to illustrate this point. Kaghan readily admitted the plays were bad — and read other passages from them proving that they were not pro- but anti-Communist.

He was hardly questioned on the original allegation brought against him two months earlier — that he had failed to obtain security clearance. The fact was, as he demonstrated, that he had obtained such clearance.

Was this man a Communist? Was he pro-Communist? Did he have Communist leanings?

This is what Ernst Reuter, the late mayor of Berlin and an old stalwart of the anti-Communist fight in the heart of Europe, had to say about Kaghan: "I remember how resolutely and how unambiguously together with us and my colleagues you have combatted every attempt at Communist infiltration."

Former Chancellor Leopold Figl of Austria, upon being apprised of the accusations, cabled Kaghan his support and inquired whether the charges were not some "April Fool's joke." For he too remembered Kaghan's effective organization of the anti-Communist propaganda machine in Vienna immediately after World War II.

Reuter and Figl clearly felt that Kaghan's valiant service on the anti-Communist barricades of Vienna and Berlin outweighed his having shared a room with a Communist in 1939.

What anti-Communist purpose was served by Senator McCarthy's attack on Theodore Kaghan? What incriminating facts were brought out? What Communist target was hit?

The answer to all these questions is: None.

The criteria of the effective anti-Communist crusade were completely violated in this case.

The hegira of Cohn and Schine

On April 4, 1953, the McCarthy hearings were in progress on television in Washington. On the same day, Roy Cohn and G. David Schine, the subcommittee's chief counsel and chief consultant, appeared in Paris. For the next ten days they scurried all over Europe.

Excluding travel time, they spent some 40 hours in Paris, 16 in Bonn, 20 in Berlin, 19 in Frankfurt, a little over 60 in Munich, 40 in Vienna, 23 in Belgrade, 24 in Athens, just over 20 in Rome, and 6 in London.

What was the purpose of this trip?

At various stops they gave different accounts of the purpose: They were looking for inefficiency, for mismanagement, for subversives, for all three. They were seeking to determine how much money had been spent "in putting across the Truman Administration" abroad. They held many hurried and hectic press conferences. They talked to very few American officials — and to some obscure Austrians and Germans. During some of their stops they spent a few fleeting moments in American information centers. In Bonn they talked with Theodore Kaghan. It was evident that this trip had something to do with the McCarthy hearings then going on.

The trip cost an estimated $8,500. What were its results? What anti-Communist purposes were served by this highly publicized junket?

No report was ever made public. Exceedingly few references to information gathered on the trip were made at the subcommittee hearings. No Communists were uncovered in the information centers abroad.

The content of the libraries

The transcript of these hearings runs to 496 pages. Of these, only 16 were given over to adverse testimony on the actual content of the overseas libraries — 10 pages of testimony by Freda Utley and 6 pages of testimony by Karl Baarslag.

Miss Utley, a journalist, testified that she found it hard to find the anti-Communist and pro-Kuomintang books, whereas numerous pro-Communist books were readily available.

Baarslag, a former official of the American Legion and later a McCarthy staff employee, made a study of the content of overseas libraries — but only in two centers, Paris and Munich. He asserted that the proportion of pro-Communist to pro-American books was about two to one. He further stated that "there were no anti-Communist magazines."

However, the State Department report pointed out that the overseas libraries subscribed to 520 publications, including just about every magazine available on American street-corners. Among them were *Life, Collier's,* the *Saturday Evening Post, Commentary,* the *Atlantic Monthly,* and hundreds of other popular American periodicals. Could all of these be considered pro-Communist?

Dr. Robert Johnson, head of the International Information Administration from February to July of 1953, wrote to Senator McCarthy in July, pointing out that the information agency had been responsible for disseminating 6,000,000 copies of anti-Communist books through its 184 libraries in 65 countries. And, referring to Baarslag's testimony, he added: "I cannot understand why anyone would deal in such patent falsehoods unless he were completely incompetent as an observer or downright malicious."

How does Senator McCarthy measure up, on the record of his investigation of the International Information Administration, to the criteria of an effective anti-Communist crusade?

The Senator in this investigation did not turn up one Communist, pro-Communist, Communist agent, stooge, dupe, or spy. He produced no evidence to substantiate his sensational, widely publicized charges of Communist infiltration, subversion, or sabotage. He presented no facts about a Communist plot. He left all of his unsubstantiated charges, allegations, and accusations suspended in mid-air — as though, once having displayed them on television, he lost all interest in them. He confused non-Communists with Communists. And he attacked well-known anti-Communists as though they were members of the very conspiracy they had fought long and successfully.

In this first of his two major investigations after he became chairman of the subcommittee, Senator McCarthy persistently failed the test of effective anti-Communism.

II. FORT MONMOUTH

Senator McCarthy's second major investigation concerned alleged subversion at Fort Monmouth.

The Army Signal Center at Fort Monmouth is one of this country's most vital defense installations. It perhaps ranks second only to the atomic installations as a center of great military and defense secrets, in the fields of radar, electronics, meteorology, and applied physics. It is the heart of America's defense preparations against atomic disaster. In addition to thousands of military personnel, the Center employs some 7,800 civilians, many hundreds of whom are highly trained and skilled scientists.

Beginning in the fall of 1953, the nation was treated to sensational charges of espionage and subversion at this great defense bastion.

By October 1953, Senator McCarthy knew — as did the rest of the country — of several suspensions at Monmouth on security grounds. He also knew that the Army's own investigation, which had begun in August under President Eisenhower's new security program and which had produced these suspensions, was continuing.

He immediately launched his own investigation in executive session. For weeks, these two inquiries continued concurrently. Shortly after the Senator had injected himself into the picture, the Army announced the suspension of 27 Monmouth employees. All told, 36 Monmouth scientists have been suspended. Four have been reinstated without charges and with full clearance restored; 10 have been reinstated without charges, but with full clearance still pending; 22 have received charges and are in security channels (as of July 1, 1954). Of these, a First Army security board has recommended dismissal in 4 cases, and the recommendations have been appealed to the Secretary of the Army.

It was Senator McCarthy's procedure that startled and electrified the nation. He held his hearings in executive session; at the conclusion of each he briefed the press on what had taken place behind his closed doors. Witnesses trooped in and out. They included employees, suspended employees, former employees — and certain persons who had been employed not at Monmouth but at private firms that did subcontracting for the Signal Corps.

Some witnesses — not identified — had, according to Senator McCarthy, pleaded the protection of the Fifth Amendment. Others, perhaps, had not. But they were all mixed in together. And the picture that seemed to emerge was one of espionage.

Here, beginning with his opening statement on October 12, 1953, is a survey of the Senator's own words on the subject:

It has all the earmarks of extremely dangerous espionage. If it develops, it may envelop the entire Signal Corps.

It appears to be a case of current espionage of an extremely dangerous nature.

[It] definitely involves espionage [relating to] our entire defense against atomic attack.

There is no question now, from the evidence, that there has been espionage in the Army Signal Corps.

We have uncovered very, very current espionage.

Senator McCarthy proceeded to document this devastating charge with lurid details — the disappearance of classified documents and their reappearance in Soviet East Germany; the breakdown of a witness, who then indicated his willingness to "tell all" about the spy ring; the discovery of classified documents at the home of one of Monmouth's most important scientists; a tie-up of the Monmouth spy ring with Julius Rosenberg, executed atomic spy.

It really appeared, on this occasion, that the Senator had struck pay dirt. He seemed to have identified, pinpointed, and exposed the enemy clearly and unmistakably. This looked like the real McCoy — an effective anti-Communist drive.

Subsequent revelations have disclosed these facts:

(1) Not one of the suspended scientists has been charged with espionage. Only two have been accused of past Communist Party affiliation, and these charges have been vigorously denied, as have all charges against all the others who were suspended. No one's loyalty has been reliably called into question.

(2) Not one of the suspended scientists has pleaded the Fifth Amendment before Senator McCarthy or the Army investigation. All claim they can prove their long-standing anti-Communism.

(3) McCarthy's other charges had all previously been thoroughly investigated by the Army, the FBI, and Congress — and they have all been exploded as utterly groundless.

(4) All of these disclosures were capped by Secretary of the Army Stevens' statements that the Army had been "unable to find anything relating to espionage" at Monmouth during the course of a thorough-going investigation. "We have got no evidence of espionage," he declared categorically in November 1953.

In February 1954 Secretary Stevens reiterated: "Insofar as the

Army has thus far been able to determine, there is no current espionage or other subversive activities at Fort Monmouth."

And again, in April and May of 1954, during the course of the special Senate investigation of the Schine case, the Secretary repeated many times that there was no evidence of espionage at Fort Monmouth.

He went even further. He declared there *was* proof of *attempted* espionage during World War II, when Julius Rosenberg had access to — and friends in — the Fort. But Stevens also stated that he did not know of any actual espionage even then.

And be it noted that during the war the Soviet military had representatives at Monmouth under Allied Lend-Lease arrangements, handling classified documents.

When Senator McCarthy finally held public hearings on Monmouth, in November and December of 1953, he called only one currently employed Monmouth scientist — who vehemently denied any past or present Communist affiliation. Thereafter the open hearings petered out. They stopped in December.

No report on the Monmouth investigation has appeared. The Senator failed to bring to light any evidence not already known and acted upon by the FBI and the Army. No Communists, pro-Communists, or spies were uncovered at Monmouth. No evidence was produced to substantiate the sensational charges that had been fed to the newspapers and the television cameras.

Why did Senator McCarthy fail to follow through on his charges of espionage in full-scale public hearings? Why did he drop the whole case and turn to other investigations? Why did he revive old charges that had been thoroughly investigated and exploded long before he entered the picture? And why — if these earlier investigations were suspect because some of them had been conducted under the Truman administration — why did he not complete and reveal the substantiated results of his own reinvestigation?

There would seem to be only one conclusion: In the Monmouth investigation, as in the International Information Administration investigation, Senator McCarthy persistently failed to measure up to the criteria of effective anti-Communist activity.

III. THE CHALLENGE TO THE ADMINISTRATION

Senator McCarthy seems unable to conclude anything he begins. There is always the gap between (a) the sensational, widely publicized allegations and (b) the consistent failure to follow through.

The record of the two major investigations in which he had a free hand demonstrates this pattern.

The pattern reveals that McCarthy has been unable to substantiate his charges or advance any solid evidence for them. But the pattern also shows that he is essentially uninterested in pursuing any case of Communist infiltration. Once having made his attack "under circumstances and at times and places of his own choosing," he loses all further interest and drops the matter.

This may well come as a shock to those who have envisaged Senator McCarthy as the apotheosis of the anti-Communist crusade. Surely the Senator is an anti-Communist. But the crux of the matter is this (to paraphrase what the Senator is wont to say to his victims): He has never proved the seriousness and substantiality of his anti-Communism.

If this analysis is correct, it really poses the question: If Senator McCarthy is not really a serious, determined, and persistent anti-Communist, why did he latch on to this popular and explosive issue?

A perusal of McCarthy's over-all record since he assumed the chairmanship of his subcommittee provides an answer:

(1) The record demonstrates a steady crescendo of attacks on President Eisenhower and his administration. The pitch becomes sharper, the tempo speedier, the tone more strident.

(2) The issue of Communism is the club wielded in these attacks.

(3) Since Senator McCarthy exploits this issue in no genuine and effective sense, his objective in exploiting it must be to achieve and retain power and renown.

Let us examine the Senator's record since the Republican administration came into office.

A. The First Target: John Foster Dulles

The Eisenhower administration had been in office hardly two weeks when McCarthy leveled a serious charge: foreign-service personnel-security files were being tampered with. He also indicated resentment at the demotion of the State Department security man who had complained to him of this alleged practice.

The man who had complained to McCarthy was immediately returned to his job.

It is true that the security people accused by McCarthy were "Acheson hang-overs" against whom he had for three years been conducting a vendetta. Still, it was rather unsettling for a new

Secretary of State to have this sort of thing thrown at his Department before he had even gotten the feel of his swivel-chair.

B. *The Second Target: Walter Bedell Smith*

During the first week of the Voice of America hearings, Senator McCarthy announced with obvious pleasure that Secretary Dulles had promised full co-operation in the investigation. But a few days later, he learned with consternation of a memorandum authorized by Under-Secretary of State Walter Bedell Smith, stating "that it is a matter of individual employee discretion as to whether he talks informally with a member of a committee or subcommittee staff without a Senator being present."

Senator McCarthy took umbrage at what he considered a reversal of Dulles' promise of co-operation. He virtually ordered General Smith to appear the same day in executive session to explain himself.

The next day the memorandum was reversed — another unsettling experience for the new administration.

C. *The Third Target: The New Team at the State Department*

In late February 1953 Scott McLeod was appointed Personnel and Security Officer for the State Department. This combination of two functions in the person of one official was a departure from previous practice. It was universally interpreted as a victory for McCarthy's views on security matters. This interpretation was strengthened by the equally universal view of McLeod as a "McCarthy man" — a view shared by the Senator himself.

The administration was not unaware of the fact that McCarthy had an official watchdog at the "new" State Department.

D. *The Bohlen Case*
Targets: Dulles, Taft, Knowland, Eisenhower

During the third week in March, when the administration had been in office only a month, the controversy over President Eisenhower's appointment of Charles Bohlen as Ambassador to Russia made front-page news.

This was shortly after the death of Stalin, and the United States had no top representative in Moscow to gauge and interpret the swift-moving events that followed.

The opposition to the appointment was at first led by Senators Bridges, Dirksen, and McCarran, on the ground that the American people could not have confidence in a man so closely associated with the Roosevelt-Truman foreign policies. This was a serious and legitimate ground for debate. But when Senator McCarthy entered the scene, the Senate's attention was swiftly diverted from the level of policy to that of "security."

McCarthy claimed to have "definitely established" that Scott McLeod had refused to clear Bohlen. He labeled as "untrue" Secretary Dulles' explanation of McLeod's position. (According to Dulles, McLeod shared Dulles' confidence in Bohlen.) The Senator undertook a cloakroom campaign of innuendo designed to embarrass Bohlen personally; this campaign culminated in McCarthy's demand that Bohlen submit to a lie-detector test. When Majority Leader Robert Taft, representing the administration, rejected the utility and feasibility of the lie detector, McCarthy renewed his attack.

Senator McCarthy reiterated his charges even *after* President Eisenhower, Senator Taft, and Senator Knowland expressed confidence in Bohlen. When McCarthy attacked the veracity of both Dulles and Knowland, the latter angrily retorted, "If we have so destroyed confidence in men in government of the United States, then God help us."

Senator McCarthy must have known — as did the administration, the Congress, and the press — that his campaign was doomed to failure when he began it. He never expected to win. The very hopelessness of his cause reflects its gratuitous nature. No more direct challenge to the authority and prestige of the Eisenhower administration, at home and abroad, could have been made.

E. The Case of the Greek Ships
Targets: Dulles, Stassen, Executive Branch

Senator McCarthy was fully prepared to cover his defeat on the Bohlen issue. On March 27, 1953, the same day the Senate confirmed Ambassador Bohlen, McCarthy announced the sensational news that he had (without the knowledge of his subcommittee colleagues) successfully negotiated an agreement with the Greek owners of 242 ships: these men agreed to stop shipments to Communist Chinese, North Korean, and Soviet Pacific ports. McCarthy spoke of the "dismal failure" of the Eisenhower administration to get results on this matter.

official but confidential sources — that the State Department had only a few weeks previously reached a similar agreement with the Greek government. It had kept the agreement secret in deference to the prestige of that government. The Greek shipowners, in agreeing to McCarthy's terms, had merely confirmed, for the sake of good public relations, their government's prior action.

The administration spokesman, Harold Stassen, openly asserted that this encroachment on Executive prerogative in foreign affairs was undermining American foreign policy. But the administration failed to sustain him in this position. However, Senator McCarthy later conceded that the Constitution reserves the conduct of foreign relations to the Executive.

But, significantly, he did not promise to abstain from any future encroachment on that right.

F. Target: James B. Conant

In June, Senator McCarthy tangled with another of President Eisenhower's recent appointees — Dr. James Conant, distinguished former president of Harvard University and the new High Commissioner in Germany. At an Appropriations Committee hearing, where Dr. Conant was testifying in support of the budget for the High Commissioner's office (HICOG), McCarthy questioned him at considerable length about his views concerning Theodore Kaghan. The Senator also quizzed Conant in detail on his views regarding the presence of Communist-authored books in American overseas libraries.

When McCarthy learned that Conant strongly defended Kaghan and did not share the Senator's views on the overseas libraries, he threatened to see that HICOG was cut off without a penny.

Conant was not an "Acheson hang-over." This was another sally against President Eisenhower's policies and personnel.

G. Small Volleys

1. The J. B. Matthews Case
Target: Eisenhower

McCarthy's appointment of J. B. Matthews as executive director of his subcommittee created a furor. Matthews had just published an article in the *American Mercury* branding "at least 7,000 Protestant clergymen" as "party members, fellow-travelers, espionage

The fact actually was — as Senator McCarthy had learned from agents, party-line adherents, and unwilling dupes" of the Communist Party. President Eisenhower made known his displeasure.

McCarthy's response was a spirited defense of his associate — who was nevertheless forced to resign.

2. The Feint at the C.I.A.
Targets: Allen Dulles, Walter Bedell Smith

When McCarthy saw that overwhelming public and official pressure would force him to accept Matthews' reluctant resignation, he had on hand a new sensation to cover his retreat and to renew his attack on the administration — a threatened investigation of the Central Intelligence Agency (C.I.A.).

The ostensible ground for investigating the C.I.A. was that one of that super-secret organization's high officials, William Bundy, a son-in-law of Dean Acheson, had contributed money for the defense of Alger Hiss. But this charge was recognized as an indirect means of attacking Walter Bedell Smith and Allen Dulles, the former and current heads of C.I.A. — both important administration officials. Only great pressure exerted by Vice President Nixon, as unofficial intermediary between McCarthy and the administration, led the Senator to desist.

3. The Issue of East-West Trade
Targets: Stassen, Dulles, Eisenhower

McCarthy had still another ace up his sleeve with which to harass the administration: the issue of East-West trade.

In late July the Senator made public a subcommittee report on the Western world's trade with Red China.[4] This report was sober, factual, detailed, and restrained. It was used by the Senator, however, as a convenient weapon in his continuing campaign against the administration's encouragement of what he called "this bloody traffic."

From August to October things were fairly quiet in Washington. The administration gratefully accepted the surcease from the Senator's pressure: he was preoccupied with his approaching wedding to his assistant, Jean Kerr.

---

[4] The report was written by Robert Kennedy, a member of the subcommittee staff who, in January 1954, was appointed counsel for the Democratic minority of the subcommittee.

H. Fort Monmouth
Targets: Stevens and the Army

In October, McCarthy interrupted his honeymoon and returned to plunge into the Fort Monmouth investigation. This investigation led him to his first big clash with Secretary of the Army Stevens.

I. The Reply to Truman
Targets: Dulles, Bedell Smith, Eisenhower,
State Department, Foreign Service

In November, Senator McCarthy heightened the pitch of his assault upon the Eisenhower administration. In the course of a nation-wide radio and television address formally billed as a reply to former President Truman,[5] McCarthy shifted the burden of his attack to the Eisenhower administration. He sharply pressed three major criticisms:

(1) He accused the administration of adhering to the Truman-Acheson pattern of sending "perfumed notes" to our allies in protest against their continued trade with Red China.

(2) He accused the administration of fumbling and deliberate delay in disposing of the John Paton Davies case. (Davies, a career diplomat in the China service and later connected with the Far Eastern Division of the State Department and with the C.I.A., had repeatedly been accused of Communist sympathies. But his old chief at the C.I.A., Walter Bedell Smith, had testified before the Senate Internal Security Subcommittee that Davies enjoyed his full confidence.)

(3) He took explicit issue with President Eisenhower's strongly stated conviction that "Communists-in-government" should not be an issue in the 1954 Congressional elections. McCarthy here came closer than ever before to a direct challenge to the President's authority. The Senator projected himself and his public career as the real issue for 1954.

---

[5] The week before, Truman had made a nationally televised defense of his record in the Harry Dexter White case. Attorney General Herbert Brownell had earlier charged that Truman retained White as Assistant Secretary of the Treasury despite several clear and urgent warnings from the FBI that White was a Communist underground agent. (Subsequent testimony before the Senate Internal Security Subcommittee substantiated the charge that the FBI warnings had not been heeded.) The Truman reply denied the charge and described it as a manifestation of "McCarthyism." Senator McCarthy immediately demanded and received equal air time to answer Truman.

A few days later Secretary Dulles, with the full approval of the President, replied sharply to the Senator, declaring that his attacks on our allies struck "at the heart of our foreign policy." But the Senator did not hesitate to take up the challenge. He made it even clearer that the issue was between the President and the Senator, saying, "I strongly urge every American who feels as I do about this blood trade with a mortal enemy to write or wire the President."

J. The Case of the Pink Dentist
Targets: The Army, Zwicker, Stevens, Eisenhower

The Peress case broke at the end of January 1954. It brought to light a confusion in Congressional legislation and in Army regulations dealing with security cases among doctors and dentists. The case also demonstrated the snail's pace traditionally attributed to bureaucratic paper-work.

Irving Peress, a New York dentist, received a captain's commission on October 15, 1952. On October 28 he filled out the regulation Army forms, including a security form with questions about membership in organizations cited as subversive by the Attorney General. In December 1952 — in a move quite unrelated to Peress or any other individual — the Army changed its rules on security forms for commissioned officers: the forms henceforth had to be filled out before, not after, commissioning.

It was not until February 1953 that it was noticed that Captain Peress had not answered the questions relating to membership in subversive organizations; an investigation of his record was immediately instituted. Meanwhile, in the normal course of Army procedure, he had been shifted from one camp to another and received orders for overseas duty. Finally, in March 1953, he was ordered to a permanent station at Camp Kilmer, New Jersey, a "compassionate" assignment allowed him so that he might be near his wife, who was ill. And his papers kept following him from one station to another.

In July 1953 a report on the completed investigation of Peress was sent to First Army Headquarters. The report recommended his dismissal. In August, Peress received an interrogatory form citing the evidence against him and requesting a reply. He refused to answer the questions, pleading the protection of the Fifth Amendment.

In October 1953 Peress, together with seven thousand other doctors and dentists in the armed forces, received a promotion.

This mass of promotions was the direct result of the enactment by Congress of an amendment to the Doctor Draft Law, providing for general readjustment upward in medical ranks to reflect more closely the doctors' status and income in civilian life.

In December 1953 an Army personnel board decided to separate Major Peress as quickly as possible. But how quickly can the Army's paper-work move? Furthermore, the Army faced other problems relating to Peress' separation. It decided, on the basis of a previous judicial precedent, that it could not court-martial him for failure to answer security questions. It had no grounds, within its regulations, for a dishonorable discharge. It feared that discharge on an "other than honorable" basis might be challenged and cause delay. It therefore finally decided that an honorable discharge would be the quickest way of getting rid of Peress. On December 30, 1953, Peress was given notice of discharge as of March 31, 1954, unless he requested it before then.

On January 30, 1954, Senator McCarthy called Peress before his subcommittee, where the dentist again invoked the Fifth Amendment. On February 1, Peress requested an immediate discharge. It was approved at once. That same day, McCarthy asked the Army to hold Peress for court-martial (which the Army had previously decided it could not do). Major Peress received his honorable discharge the following day.

Here was a classic combination of loopholes in laws and regulations and administrative slowness. But Senator McCarthy viewed the matter differently. He made it the basis of the charge that the Army was "coddling" Communists. When General Ralph Zwicker, commandant of Camp Kilmer, refused, on the basis of a Presidential directive, to give the names of Army personnel involved in Peress' promotion and honorable discharge, McCarthy impugned Zwicker's loyalty.

McCarthy was right in contending that Peress should not have been in the Army. But he completely ignored the fact that the Army itself had felt the same way and had begun to take action on the case a year before the Senator came on the scene. Far from coddling Communists, the Army acted — in a slow-footed way, to be sure — to discharge Peress.

It was clear at the time, and it became explicit during the hearings on the Army-McCarthy imbroglio, that this case brought the Senator's conflict with the administration to a head. Starting with a renewed attack on his old enemy, the Army, he proceeded from a violent diatribe against a distinguished general to forcing the unwary Secretary Stevens into an inadvertent capitulation — and to another open confrontation with the President.

It was this clash that finally led to the degrading spectacle of a whole nation — its Congress, its military and defense leaders, its press, radio, and television — involved in a raging squabble, at precisely the time when it should have been contemplating the disastrous prospect of Allied disunity in the face of renewed Communist aggression.

Since the spring of 1953, Senator McCarthy has been stepping up the tempo and pitch of his challenge to the Eisenhower administration and the authority of the President. This is clearly related to his record prior to 1953, for the fulcrum of his attack on Eisenhower and Truman has been identical: the issue of Communists in government.

The Senator seized upon a sure-fire issue at precisely the right national-psychological moment — 1950. He could have made of the issue a potent weapon in the national defense. But the record shows that he has consistently ignored, by-passed, and slighted the criteria of an effective fight against the Communist threat.

Senator McCarthy has not been particularly successful in putting his finger on Communist infiltration. But he has been brilliantly successful in exploiting that issue as an instrument for enhancing his own power and status. This has led him to maintain a persistent drumfire of assault on the Eisenhower administration as the climax of his whole career. It has, finally, resulted in a direct challenge to the President himself for the leadership of the Republican Party.

But McCarthy presents a problem to the whole nation, not just to the Republican Party, for his essentially cynical manipulation of this issue has engaged him in the tactics of deceit and in a radical, anti-conservative political strategy. Both the tactics and the strategy can only be destructive of the ends sought by authentic anti-Communists.

3. The Methods

Polonius: Though this be madness, yet there's method in't.
  Will you walk out of the air, my lord?
Hamlet: Into my grave.

SHAKESPEARE

Much of the popular support that has made Senator McCarthy a formidable force in American politics comes from those who declare that because they approve the Senator's professed goal of combatting Communism, they feel obliged to condone the admitted roughness and toughness of his methods.

One difficulty with this point of view is that its adherents, when pressed, cannot always articulate in concrete terms what the Senator's so-called methods are. Before we can approve or disapprove of Joseph McCarthy's methods, we have to know and evaluate them, as we must know and evaluate all political methods and their relation to the ends they are designed to serve.

Senator McCarthy contends that the end he strives for is the ending of the Communist infiltration and subversion that would destroy democracy in the United States. The Communists say that their end, as expressed by the "Internationale," is to "free the prisoners of starvation," to realize the dream of utopian socialism.

In practice, Communism turns out to be not a goal, but a way of life. The means become the end.

With this, the most terrible lesson of recent history, before us, we are compelled to test and compare all political methods and means with those of totalitarianism in order to determine their appropriateness to democracy and to weigh carefully the results these means have produced, or are likely to produce in the future. Foresight is the great weapon of popular intelligence in a democracy.

Fortunately, Communist methods of political controversy,[1] the

---

[1] Communist methods other than those of political controversy include, of course, the institutionalization of slave labor, brain-washing, torture, man-made starvation on a mass scale, and the bullet in the back of the head.

basis of comparison here, are no secret. Among them, ten are most easily discernible as consistent patterns:

1. The multiple untruth
2. The abuse of documents
3. Insinuation and innuendo
4. The slander amalgam
5. Intimidation
6. Attributing significance to the irrelevant
7. The bluff and the diversionary gambit
8. The personal spy network
9. Contempt for the law
10. The unfounded charge of treason

It is unnecessary to dwell at length on Communist methods. The methods of Communists are relevant here only as the touchstones of other methods. It has been argued that most men in politics use devious means to achieve their ends. But to some politicians — Communists, Fascists, perhaps others — lies and deceit become the very stuff of politics, to be used constantly in the achievement of the goal. "A Communist," wrote Lenin in 1920 in a letter addressed to the American working class, "must be prepared to make every sacrifice . . . resort to all sorts of schemes and stratagems, employ illegitimate methods, conceal the truth."

A few illustrations may be useful.

1. The multiple untruth

In 1952 and 1953 the Communists charged that thousands of Chinese and North Koreans were sick with dread diseases caused by American germ warfare. It is true that many people in Communist territory were sick. It is true that their diseases were caused by germs. But it is not true that American planes dropped these germs. Out of a half-truth, the Communists concocted a big lie, which they then repeated endlessly.

2. The abuse of documents

During the Moscow trials, the prosecution made repeated references to "documents" incriminating Trotsky and his associates, but no such documents were ever made part of the record.

Doctoring of photographs has long been an art in the Soviet Union. Although Lenin and Trotsky were together the prime movers behind the Russian revolution, the photographs of official

Soviet histories have been altered to show, at Lenin's side, not Trotsky but Stalin.

Malenkov has also resorted to pictorial falsification. At the signing of the Soviet-China pact of 1950, a photo was taken showing Molotov and Vishinsky next to Stalin and Mao, with Malenkov in the background. The month Stalin died, the picture reappeared in *Pravda* — cropped and altered to show Malenkov *alone* with Stalin and Mao.

3. Insinuation and innuendo

Communists invariably insinuate that their opponents are criminals and enemies of mankind. Thus, when they called democratic socialists "social-fascists," they insinuated that the socialists are merely a different shade of fascist. When they call Western leaders "warmongers," the Communists imply not merely that the West would use war for its own aggrandizement but that the Soviet Union is the only defender of peace.

4. The slander amalgam

The Communists time and again resort to slander by lumping people of different stripes in the same category or unjustly associating innocent persons with dishonorable persons or causes. During the 1930's, democratic socialists in the United States, long in the vanguard of the fight against both Communism and Fascism, were, as we have already said, constantly vilified by the Communists as "social-fascists." In the next decade, when President Harry Truman displeased the Kremlin, the Soviet *Literary Gazette* said, "The haberdasher . . . is striving for the laurels of the corporal from Munich," maliciously bracketing Truman with Hitler.

5. Intimidation

The entire state apparatus of Communist totalitarianism is a form of institutionalized intimidation. People living under Communism are constantly being intimidated — and their thoughts and actions influenced — by the presence of spies for the secret police, by the possibility of being arrested without cause, by the fact that an accusation implies guilt, by the bullying of witnesses in court, and by the constant threat of being forced to join the millions of slave laborers.

6. Attributing significance to the irrelevant

Nicolai Krylenko was an important Soviet prosecutor in the 1920's, and in the 1930's he became Soviet Commissar of Justice. Krylenko was never a member of a "deviationist" group and always slavishly followed Stalin's political line. Nevertheless, when Stalin made a speech in March 1935 — a speech that had nothing to do with Krylenko — Andrei Vishinsky wrote an article on that speech, making it seem as if Stalin and Krylenko were at odds with each other. Krylenko said Stalin's speech had nothing to do with him. Replied Vishinsky:

First of all, let us dwell on the question which is of enormous importance, though it does not have a direct relation to the discussion. The question concerns Comrade Krylenko's assertion that the problems of principle concerning our policy of criminal law and court proceedings should not be linked with Comrade Stalin's historically important speech of March 4th. Is this assertion of Comrade Krylenko correct? It seems to me that the *mere fact of raising this question* is sufficient to make entirely obvious Comrade Krylenko's profound error.

Krylenko was then accused of past errors (of which he had already publicly repented), purged, and executed.

7. The bluff and the diversionary gambit

The bluff is a standard device of Communist diplomacy. For example, in 1945 the Soviet Union denounced its treaties of neutrality and friendship with Turkey, demanding control of the Dardanelles and other territorial concessions. This Soviet bluff was called by Turkey, with the backing of the United States — and Moscow retreated from its demands.

In 1946, the Soviet Union sought, by infiltration and bluster, to detach the province of Azerbaijan from Iran and absorb it into the Soviet Union. Iran called this bluff by appealing to the United Nations Security Council, which forced the Soviets to withdraw.

In 1948, the Soviets attempted to force the American, British, and French forces out of their sectors of occupied Berlin. The Soviet army of occupation applied this pressure by cutting highway and rail communications with the city. When the Berlin airlift called the Soviet bluff, the Communists ceased to contest the right of the Western powers to stay in Berlin.

8. The personal spy network

Personal spy networks are part and parcel of the struggle for political power in Communist states. In the 1940's and early 1950's, the secret police, a corps of spies supposedly loyal to Beria, was in turn infiltrated by personal spies, first of Stalin, then of Malenkov. In the Soviet Union and its satellites, even children are recruited into an omnipresent spy system and obliged to spy on their parents.

9. Contempt for the law

Communists break the laws of non-Communist countries whenever it suits them to do so. Hiss and his confederates stole secret documents. Browder traveled on a forged passport. At the same time, the Party employs all the resources of the law in behalf of Communist defendants, as during the trial of top Party leaders in the United States under the Smith Act.

The Soviet Union has an elaborate system of law embodying theoretical protections to the Soviet citizen — which the NKVD violates habitually. Arrest without warrant, conviction without trial, and long sentences to slave-labor camps are what any Soviet citizen must expect — and what millions have experienced — from the Soviet state in violation of its own constitution.

10. The unfounded charge of treason

In Communist countries any public criticism of the regime is considered treasonable, and an elaborate system of spies and stool pigeons makes even private criticism dangerous. The defendants in the Moscow trials were accused, not of organizing opposition to Stalin (of which they may well have been guilty), but of conspiring with German and Japanese agents to betray the Soviet Union to Hitler and the Mikado. In Czechoslovakia, when Premier Gottwald and his Moscow overlords needed a scapegoat on whom to blame the scarcity of food and consumer goods, Party Secretary Rudolph Slansky was accused and convicted, not of responsibility for these failures of the regime, but of treasonable conspiracy with British and American agents. Frequently, in all Communist police states, the most trivial offense — such as a mother's theft of a bit of food for her hungry children — becomes "treasonable sabotage against the State."

Since Senator McCarthy hates and opposes Communism, we might reasonably assume not only that he would oppose its methods but that he would disdain and forswear their use by himself and by his aides and supporters. It is rather startling, therefore, to find that during his relatively brief political career, the Junior Senator from Wisconsin has employed not some but all of these methods — and not once or twice but habitually.

I. THE MULTIPLE UNTRUTH

Multiple untruth: A combination of truth, half-truth, and whole cloth, subtly interwoven and frequently repeated in the same or somewhat revised form, especially in the face of contradictory evidence.

A. *The Claim of Success in the State Department*

In an interview with the *U.S. News and World Report* in September 1951, Senator McCarthy claimed responsibility for rooting out of the State Department a number of well-known Communists. He said: "We got Alger Hiss out, we got Marzani out, Wadleigh, George Shaw Wheeler, and a few others."

It is certainly true that these men were Communists. It is also true that by 1951 they were all out of government.

However:

(1) Alger Hiss resigned from the State Department in February 1947 — just three years before McCarthy began his anti-Communist activities. The facts concerning Hiss were brought out by the House Committee on Un-American Activities, in which the then Representative Richard Nixon played the chief role. And Hiss was prosecuted by President Truman's Justice Department two years before McCarthy's Wheeling speech.

(2) Carl Aldo Marzani was fired in 1946 — a month before McCarthy took his seat in the Senate. He was subsequently prosecuted successfully by President Truman's Justice Department for perjury in denying his Communist affiliations.

(3) Julian Wadleigh left the State Department in 1946 and had been publicly exposed as an espionage agent by Whittaker Chambers two years before the Wheeling speech.

(4) George Shaw Wheeler left the State Department in 1947, under fire of a departmental security investigation.

Who were the "few others" the Senator claimed in 1951? He never said.

But in 1952 the Senator tried to take credit for the successful investigation and conviction of William Remington. (In 1952 the Senator compiled a new list of claimed victories to his credit, including Remington; none of these had appeared in his 1951 list.)

The fact is, as Senator Ferguson had already written in 1951, that ". . . outside of Senator McCarthy's general statements of Communism in government, which of course embraced Remington, I personally do not know of any particular work he did in the Remington case."

B. The Claim of Success in the Voice of America

On May 28, 1954, Roy Cohn, testifying before the Senate subcommittee investigating the Army-McCarthy controversy, stated that the Voice of America investigation had been "the most important one" conducted by Senator McCarthy in 1953. McCarthy and Cohn were looking, they constantly contended, for Communist infiltrators and subversives in the information program. And they repeatedly intimated that their investigation had succeeded.

As we showed in Chapter 2, they found in the Voice of America no Communists, no pro-Communists, no subversives, no persons of questionable loyalty, and no security risks.

C. The Claim of Success at Fort Monmouth

On May 4, 1954, Secretary of the Army Robert T. Stevens, testifying before the Senate investigating subcommittee, stated, as we have already noted, that to his knowledge there were no Communists working at the Army's Signal Center at Fort Monmouth. He also stated that no Monmouth employee had invoked the Fifth Amendment — that none had claimed that his truthful testimony would tend to incriminate him.

Senator McCarthy's response was quick and hot-tempered:

McCARTHY. . . . When the Secretary of the Army makes . . . a statement which is so clearly false, known to us to be false, the only way I can correct it is to pick up a few of the individual cases which show that he is not speaking the truth.

The Senator went on to refer to

. . . a Ruth Levine, who had top-secret clearance in telecommunications . . . was subpoenaed December 13 [1953], appeared December 16, and took the Fifth Amendment as to conspiracy to commit espionage. I don't think you want to make that misstatement of fact, Mr. Secretary.

This was not the first time the Senator had referred to the Levine case. On February 2, 1954, in the course of a Senate debate in which he sought to justify a renewed appropriation of $214,000 for his committee, McCarthy offered to "recount some evidence of very current espionage at Fort Monmouth." He referred to Ruth Levine as "a Federal employee" who "had been an employee of the telecommunications office and had been handling Fort Monmouth radar material."

What were the facts in the case?

Ruth Levine, as Senator McCarthy correctly stated, had been subpoenaed on December 13. Furthermore she resigned her job immediately after accepting the subpoena. She appeared before the McCarthy committee in public session, and she did "take the Fifth Amendment" regarding conspiracy to commit espionage (although she denied ever having actually committed it).

Here, indeed, was a case of apparently lax security procedures. And it can justly be said that Senator McCarthy performed a service in indirectly leading to her resignation.

But there was only one small thing wrong with the way the Senator presented the case: Ruth Levine was not and never had been an employee of the Army at Fort Monmouth.

Senator McCarthy, however, not content with his success in getting rid of a "Fifth Amendment Communist," wanted to give the false impression that Ruth Levine had been a Fort Monmouth employee.

She had, in fact, been an employee of the Federal Telecommunications Laboratory, a private company, a subsidiary of the International Telephone and Telegraph Corporation. This was the factual basis on which the Senator strung out a whole series of falsehoods over a period of several months, during which he called her "a Federal employee," "an employee of the telecommunications office" who had "top-secret clearance in telecommunications."

D. The Matthews Affair

Here was another instance of bald misrepresentation of the facts.

In July 1953 a storm broke over McCarthy's hiring of J. B. Matthews as his Committee's research director. The three Democratic members of the subcommittee resigned when the Senator forced through a vote vesting in him the sole power to hire and fire staff members. As Senators McClellan, Symington, and Jackson put it at the time, they were placed in "the impossible position of having responsibility without any voice, right or authority."

McCarthy's reaction was swift. "If they don't want," he said, "to take part in uncovering the graft and corruption of the old Truman-Acheson administration, they are, of course, entitled to refuse."

A few days later, the Wisconsin Senator reiterated this version of the facts, and added a new twist. He said he would not seek to have the Democrats return if they felt that as Senators "they wanted to draw their pay and not do their work."

This is a somewhat subtler manifestation of the multiple untruth in action. In the first place, McCarthy implied that his Democratic colleagues were not doing their duty as Senators. Secondly, quite by indirection, he skillfully defined that duty as the uncovering of graft and corruption in the Truman administration.

Wholly aside from the question of whether graft and corruption did or did not exist in the Truman administration, there is, of course, nothing in the public record to indicate that McCarthy was uncovering anything of the sort.

E. Truman on "McCarthyism"

In his televised reply to former President Truman's attack on him in November 1953, the Senator claimed that Mr. Truman's definition of "McCarthyism" was "identical, word for word, comma for comma," with that of the Communist *Daily Worker*. The intended impression was obvious — that Truman had used a Communist source for his attack on McCarthy.

But the next day the United Press reported that the Senator's office could not cite the issue of the *Daily Worker* that contained the definition of "McCarthyism." In fact, it had not appeared in any issue — but had been woven together from scattered words taken by the Senator himself from various issues of the *Daily Worker*.

F. The Owen Lattimore Case

In the spring of 1950 Senator McCarthy told the Tydings committee that Owen Lattimore was "definitely an espionage agent . . . one of the top espionage agents . . . the top Russian spy . . . the key man in a Russian espionage ring."

And he added: "I am willing to stand or fall on this one."

The Tydings committee did not even pretend to investigate these or any other charges against Owen Lattimore. Indeed the committee openly collaborated with him and his counsel, and ultimately, in its report, completely exonerated him of all suspicion.

Two years later the McCarran committee, under the able guidance of its chief counsel, Robert Morris, did investigate charges against Lattimore, as part of its investigation of the Institute of Pacific Relations. It issued a factual, devastating report on Lattimore's shabby performance as a fellow-traveler of long standing. It said: "Owen Lattimore was, from some time beginning in the 1930's, a conscious, articulate instrument of the Soviet conspiracy." An analysis of Lattimore's books and articles and of his record as editor of the Institute's *Pacific Affairs* demonstrates that he was a clever apologist for the Soviet Union, a faithful propagandist and follower of the Party line.

But this fact did not make him a spy, or the chief Soviet espionage agent — nor did anyone testify to this effect before the McCarran committee.

McCarthy had made this sensational charge at a critical point in the hearings before the Tydings committee. He was being laughed out of court by his presentation of such people as Dorothy Kenyon as "Communists." The worst that could ever have been said of such people was that they were foolish dupes at an early stage in their careers; they later proved their anti-Communism by their deeds. The Senator needed something to revive interest. Hence the Lattimore charge. When he no longer needed this sensation, he dropped it, in favor of a milder version.

G. The Malmedy Investigation

Lest it be assumed that Senator McCarthy restricts his use of distortion — the multiple untruth — to his "crusade" against Communism, we shall cite the case of the Malmedy investigation of 1949.

In 1946, 73 German SS men were tried as war criminals for having massacred American troops at Malmedy during the Battle of the Bulge, 43 of them received death sentences. In 1948 and 1949 reports began to circulate that these men had been subjected to horrible brutalities by American investigators in the case. Their appeal was taken to Army Secretary Kenneth C. Royall, who stayed their execution and ordered a special judicial investigation of the charges. In April 1949 a Senate Armed Services subcommittee opened special hearings into the whole case.

Senator McCarthy was not a member of the Armed Services Committee; but, exercising his Senatorial prerogative, he sat in as a guest of the subcommittee and soon dominated the hearings. What impelled him to inject himself into this case? Perhaps it was the votes of some of Wisconsin's German-Americans who had never reconciled themselves to America's two wars with Germany.

Here the pattern of the multiple untruth emerges clearly: the assertion of a fact that is not a fact, the repetition of the distortion, the emendation of the original statement while insisting that it is the same statement. Here are some examples from the testimony. (Senator Baldwin, Republican of Connecticut, presided over the hearing; on the witness stand was Justice Gordon Simpson, one of the members of the judicial commission appointed by Secretary Royall.)

SENATOR MCCARTHY. You knew it was claimed that these men sentenced to death were crippled for life because they had been kicked in the genitals. Didn't you think it was important to send a doctor to examine two or three of those men?

MR. SIMPSON. I suppose I saw it and forgot it, since you say it is there. I never saw a claim that a man had been injured for life because of a blow in the genitals.

SENATOR MCCARTHY. Didn't you read over Colonel Everett's affidavit? [Everett had been appointed by the Army as defense counsel for the SS men.]

MR. SIMPSON. Is it in his affidavit?

SENATOR MCCARTHY. It is in these documents, I would say, 10 or 15 times in the documents supporting Everett's application. I do wish you would look these over and discover what you have overlooked.

Meanwhile a subcommittee staff member, a Mr. Chambers, had examined the affidavits:

SENATOR BALDWIN. Mr. Chambers just advises me that an examination of Colonel Everett's affidavit, which was filed in the Supreme Court, and which was the one which was referred to here, apparently shows no claim that there was any number of men or any at all who were damaged or injured in private parts as the results of the conduct of the investigators for the prosecution. Is that correct? . . .

SENATOR MCCARTHY. Just so we don't get Mr. Chambers or anyone else in a misstatement, the affidavits filed by Colonel Everett and supporting documents set forth very definitely the physical violence used in order to get confessions.

MR. CHAMBERS. That is correct.

SENATOR MCCARTHY. Let's not distort the record. . . .

MR. CHAMBERS. Mr. Chairman, the point that I took a look at this record, as did Senator McCarthy's counsel, was to resolve the point that seemed to be in issue between Judge Simpson and Senator Mc-Carthy, in which Judge Simpson said he did not recall having seen a charge of 139 or some such number of people being ruined for life by being kicked in the testicles. In an effort to clarify that particular point, I have checked through here and it is not in the record, and I believe Mr. McCarthy's counsel will concur in that.

SENATOR MCCARTHY. All but 2 out of 139. . . . I saw it there, and there is no question about the fact that Colonel Everett's affidavit sets forth in detail the physical beatings and the type of punishment used in order to get the confessions.

MR. CHAMBERS. That is correct.

SENATOR MCCARTHY. Good.

MR. CHAMBERS. Colonel Everett's petition before the Supreme Court alleged many different types of pressures, among which were beatings, brutality, mock trials, and things of that kind.

SENATOR MCCARTHY. Teeth being kicked out, genitals being ruined, it is all in the affidavits.

MR. CHAMBERS. There is nothing on the latter point. That is the point I am trying to make.

Senator McCarthy used the same gambit in interrogating Lieutenant Perl, one of the accused Army investigators. In addition, he insinuated that the witness was lying:

SENATOR MCCARTHY. . . . Did he [one of the SS men], while on the stand, claim to the court he had been *beaten* and *mistreated?* [Italics added.]

LIEUTENANT PERL. No sir.

SENATOR MCCARTHY. You are certain of that?

LIEUTENANT PERL. Yes.

SENATOR MCCARTHY. You are sure?

MR. PERL. I read the trial record last night again.

A few minutes later, McCarthy reverted to this exchange:

SENATOR MCCARTHY. In view of your statement, Mr. Perl, that this man never claimed on the stand during the trial that he had been *mistreated* [italics added], I want to refresh your memory, if I may.

The Senator then quoted from the testimony of the person being discussed. This man claimed he had been verbally abused, but not that he had been beaten.

SENATOR MCCARTHY. In view of the fact that he did so testify, do you want to change your testimony in which you said that on the stand he made no claim he had been *mistreated,* or do you not consider that mistreatment. . . . I now have read to you from the record. I ask you in view of that, do you want to change your statement that having read the record, you find that he never made any claims of *mistreatment?* [Italics added.]

LIEUTENANT PERL. I believe, sir, that I spoke of *beating* here yesterday. [Italics added.]

In all of these cases the multiple untruth has been at work — the combination of truth, half-truth, and whole cloth, with changed terms slipped in and insinuations inserted in a casual, offhand, but very meaningful manner.

For the record it should be stated here that these charges of brutality were subsequently found to be wholly false — skillfully propagated by both neo-Nazi and Communist agents in Germany. At a subsequent hearing of the Armed Services subcommittee in Germany, a notorious Communist agent, Dr. Rudolph Aschenhauer, admitted that he had worked up the whole case in defense of the SS men, that he had manufactured all the charges — and that he was the source of the data on which the Senator based his case.

II. THE ABUSE OF DOCUMENTS

The use of documents: To bolster a case by presenting factual evidence based on authentic documents.

The abuse of documents: To give the misleading impression of using factual evidence based on authentic documents. Specifically, to take phrases out of their documentary context and thus distort the entire meaning of the facts and of the document.

A. The Mysterious Case of Calvin Coolidge

In September 1952, during the Presidential election campaign, Senator McCarthy warned the country it should not be misled into believing that there were no longer Communists in government. As evidence to the contrary, he stated:

I have in my hand the brief prepared by seven lawyers of the Justice Department dated July 28, 1952. Let me read to you from it:

"Illegal passports have been used to expedite travel in foreign countries by members of the Communist Party. Plans have been discussed by leading members of the Party and agents of the Soviet secret police to obtain blank American passports . . . from Communists employed in the State Department."

For the benefit of the press, that's on page 91 of their very excellent and lengthy brief.

A few days later Attorney General James McGranery set the record straight. The report was based on a statement by Paul Crouch, a former Communist. Crouch stated that he had — in

1928 — met a member of the Soviet secret police who told him of plans at that time to try to obtain blank passports from Communists employed in the State Department, if they could find such employees.

There was, of course, no evidence that Communists were working in Calvin Coolidge's State Department. Senator McCarthy knew that the document referred to purported plans of 1928. He conveniently neglected to mention the year in his campaign speech twenty-four years later.

B. Dean Acheson and the "New Day" in Asia

In his book *McCarthyism: The Fight For America,* published in 1952, the Senator charged that former Secretary of State Dean Acheson had "hailed the Communist victory in China as 'a new day which has dawned in Asia.' "

Secretary Acheson did indeed refer, in a speech before the National Press Club on January 12, 1950, to "a new day which has dawned in Asia." However, he described the "new day" in these terms:

Since the end of the war in Asia, we have seen over 500 million people gain their independence and over seven new nations come into existence in this area. We have the Philippines with 20 million citizens. We have Pakistan, India, Ceylon and Burma with 400 million citizens, southern Korea with 20 million citizens, and within the last few weeks, the United States of Indonesia with 75 million. . . .

As for "Communist victory," Acheson went on to say:

Communism is the most subtle instrument of Soviet foreign policy that has ever been devised; and it is really the spearhead of Russian imperialism which would, if it could, take from these people what they have won, what we want them to keep and develop, which is their own national independence, their own development of their own resources for their own good, and not as mere tributary states to this great Soviet Union.

C. The Assault on Adlai Stevenson

Senator McCarthy's abuse of documents received perhaps its most extensive work-out in his campaign attack on Adlai Stevenson in October 1952. In the short space of a half-hour of radio and television time, the Senator distorted the meaning of six separate documents in citing four instances in which he alleged Stevenson had aided the Communists.

1. Stevenson and the Merchant Marine

McCarthy charged that Stevenson, while serving as a wartime aide to Secretary of the Navy Frank Knox, had forced the retention of Communist radio operators on merchant ships.

The charge was made on the basis of a statement by Admiral Adolphus Staton, who wanted the Communist radio operators removed. According to Staton, Stevenson dissented.

But, in the same statement, Staton made it perfectly clear that Stevenson had no responsibility in the matter. Stevenson authorized the retention of these men on the basis of a memorandum from President Roosevelt, who contended (in 1943) that membership in the Communist Party was not sufficient to deprive a radio operator of his job. Stevenson, according to the Admiral, was merely passing the order along.

But the Senator carefully refrained from quoting *this* part of Admiral Staton's report.

2. Stevenson and the Daily Worker

"I hold in my hand," the Senator boomed to his television audience, "a photostat of the *Daily Worker* of October 19, 1952. . . . They refer to and quote their hatred of Eisenhowerism and then go on to say that they do not like Stevenson too well either, but that if Communists want to vote for Stevenson — O.K., vote for him."

The fact is that there was nothing on the page photostated, or on the continuation of the story on the inside pages of the *Daily Worker* (not photostated), or in any other issue of that newspaper that even remotely suggested that Communists should vote for Stevenson. In fact the Communists fought Stevenson harder than Eisenhower, because, according to their version, Stevenson paraded as a liberal and was therefore able to camouflage his reactionary motives more cleverly than the openly conservative Eisenhower.

This is how Father Robert C. Hartnett, editor of *America,* the Jesuit weekly, characterized this McCarthy attack: "That Senator McCarthy, *without a shred of warrant,* set out to smear the reputation of Governor Stevenson by trying to wrap up his candidacy in *The Daily Worker* seems to this writer, in view of the evidence, simply incontrovertible."

3. Stevenson and the Institute of Pacific Relations

In the same campaign address the Senator went on to say:

> While you may think that there can be no connection between the debonair Democratic candidate and a dilapidated Massachusetts barn, I want to show you a picture of this barn and explain the connection. Here is the outside of the barn . . . at Lee, Massachusetts. It looks as though it couldn't house a farmer's cow or goat. Here's the inside. A beautiful panelled conference room with maps of the Soviet Union. Which way does Stevenson tie up with that?
>
> My — my investigators went out and took pictures of the barn after we had been tipped off what was in it. Tipped off that there was in this barn all the missing documents from the Communist front, IPR. The IPR which was named by the McCarran Committee, named before the McCarran Committee as a cover-up for Communist espionage.
>
> Let's take a look at the photostat of the documents taken from the Massachusetts barn. One of those documents which was never supposed to see the light of day. Rather interesting it is. This is a document which shows that Alger Hiss and Frank Coe recommended Adlai Stevenson to the Mount Tremblant Conference which was called for the purpose of establishing foreign policy, postwar policy in Asia.
>
> As you know, Alger Hiss is a convicted traitor. Frank Coe is a man who has been named under oath before the Congressional Committee seven times as a member of the Communist Party.
>
> Why, why Hiss and Coe find that Adlai Stevenson is the man they want representing them at this conference, I don't know. Perhaps Adlai does.

This statement warrants careful analysis because it is an extraordinary illustration of a combination of a number of the Senator's methods discussed in this chapter — not only the abuse of documents but the multiple untruth, insinuation and innuendo, the slander amalgam, the exaggeration of the irrelevant, the unfounded charge (or implication) of treason.

Let us examine this passage in some detail.

The first step is to set the stage. The Senator does this at once by introducing the tension of an apparent paradox at the very outset. He's going to show the "connection between the debonair Democratic candidate and a dilapidated Massachusetts barn."

The suspense is heightened by the introduction of an authentic document: the photograph of "the outside of the barn."

Tension is partially relieved by the apparent innocence of the outside of the barn. "It looks as though it couldn't house a farmer's cow or goat."

But no — the innocence is deceptive. Another authentic document is flashed before the audience: a photograph of the inside of the barn. It is a "conference room with maps of the Soviet Union." Tension is heightened again by the contrast between the innocent appearance of the outside of the barn and the suspicious appearance of the inside.

A sinister element has been injected into the story, with overtones of secret Soviet machinations. Up to this point the audience has been led swiftly, and chiefly by implication, from an initial paradox to a sinister mystery.

At just this point, the innuendo is strengthened by a provocative question: "Which way does Stevenson tie up with that?"

By now Stevenson's "connection" with the innocent-looking barn seems to have become a connection with a Communist front. But this is only the beginning.

The Senator then goes on to refer to "the IPR which was named by the McCarran Committee — named before the McCarran Committee as a cover-up for Communist espionage." Here we have it out in the open: Stevenson, insinuates McCarthy, is connected with Communist espionage.

(The McCarran committee did *not* name the Institute of Pacific Relations as a "cover-up for Communist espionage." It called the Institute a "vehicle used by the Communists to orientate American Far Eastern objectives toward Communist objectives." This, of course, is insidious enough. The McCarran committee did in fact show that the Institute was infiltrated with Communists and Communist-sympathizers who frequently used their positions to influence American policy. But this does not mean that the Institute was a cover for espionage.)

Having by innuendo, insinuation and untruth established a background of conspiracy and secrecy, and having associated Stevenson with Communist espionage, the Senator proceeds to pin down the charge by abusing a document. "This is a document," he says, "which shows that Alger Hiss and Frank Coe recommended Adlai Stevenson" to a conference called for the purpose of "establishing foreign policy . . . in Asia."

By now Stevenson is associated not only with Communist espionage, but with espionage directed at subverting American foreign policy in Asia.

The web of insinuation is drawn tighter by the use of the slander amalgam — the connection of Stevenson with Coe and Hiss. And just in case his auditors have forgotten who these two are, McCarthy reminds them that "Hiss is a convicted traitor" and Coe "has been named under oath . . . seven times as a member of the Communist Party."

The final, leading rhetorical question — strengthened by the dramatic double use of "Why, why" — suggests only one answer. Why did Hiss, a convicted traitor, and Coe, accused of being a member of the Communist apparatus, want Stevenson to "represent them"? The implication of treason is unmistakable. It is strengthened by the gratuitous use of the phrase "representing them."

The charge is finally driven home to the audience by the sinister implications of the concluding sentence, an indirect answer to the leading question: "Perhaps Adlai knows."

At this point we should turn to the Institute of Pacific Relations document that the Senator abused. A perusal of the document will also reveal how McCarthy attributes significance to the irrelevant.

In the opinion of Hiss, Coe and Despres, we ought to try to get Berle or Acheson or both. . . . Another possibility we might consider is someone from Knox's office or Stimson's. Coe and Hiss mentioned Adlai Stevens [sic], one of Knox's special assistants. Hiss also suggested with some approval Harvey Bundy, former Assistant Secretary of State (under Hoover) and now special assistant to Stimson.

Then there is General Little, a Marine General formerly in China, now retired.(?) Also General Magruder, whereabouts unknown. Despres also suggested Admiral Hart, saying that it wouldn't be a bad idea to have someone who would give a pretty forthright and orthodox Navy view, as this view will greatly influence the post-war settlement.

That's the whole document.

Obviously, no more significance attaches to the recommendation of "Stevens" (Stevenson) than to that of Dean Acheson, Adolph A. Berle, and the other men mentioned. (Berle, then Assistant Secretary of State, was the man to whom Whittaker Chambers turned in 1939 to reveal the facts of the Communist underground in the government. Berle tried vainly to impress President Roosevelt with the importance of Chambers' information. Berle was then and has remained a distinguished anti-Communist liberal.)

Senator McCarthy knew, when he drew his bead on the Democratic Presidential candidate, that Adlai Stevenson had no more to do with that red barn in Massachusetts than did John Foster Dulles, Senator Homer Ferguson, Henry Luce, and Herbert Hoover — all of whom, like Stevenson, were members of the Institute of Pacific Relations.

But the Senator also knew that few in his audience had ever

bothered or ever would bother to read the transcript of the hearings of the McCarran committee.

One more point: Adlai Stevenson never did attend that conference.

4. *Stevenson and the Italian Communists*

In the same campaign speech, Senator McCarthy said:

Stevenson says, "I was the man who formulated [our post-war Italian] policy". . . and the head of the Central Intelligence Agency [General Walter Bedell Smith] says the policy then was to "connive" to put Communists into the Italian government, "connive" to bring Togliatti, the Communist leader, back from Moscow, which they did. Now I wonder what their defense of Stevenson's plans for foisting the Communists upon the Italians will be.

This bit of chicanery is as neat as the abuse of the Institute of Pacific Relations document. Here the Senator abused not one but three separate and distinct documents.

(a) An unauthorized campaign biography of Stevenson by Noel Busch became McCarthy's authority for the statement that Stevenson claimed to have formulated American policy for post-war Italy.

Stevenson never made any such claim. The unofficial biography at no point quoted him to that effect. Thus, putting that statement in quotation marks was an outright falsehood.

(b) The document on which the McCarthy charge was based was a report Stevenson had made as head of a Foreign Economic Administration study group in Italy in 1943. The report dealt with problems of economic reconstruction for post-war Italy.

There is not one word in the report about Communism or about Togliatti. Not only does the report not recommend putting the Communists into the Italian government — but it does not even touch on the problem of the government of post-war Italy. The report dealt only with economic questions, with problems of reconstruction.

Thus the statement that Stevenson "connived" to put the Communists in power in Italy is another bald lie.

(c) The third document the Senator abused was the book *My Three Years in Moscow* by General Walter Bedell Smith, at that time head of the Central Intelligence Agency, earlier our Ambassador to the Soviet Union (and later Under-Secretary of State).

At no point in this book did General Smith say that American policy in Italy was to "connive" to put the Communists into the

Italian government. McCarthy's statement to this effect is another untruth.

Nor did Smith ever mention Adlai Stevenson in that book. What he did say was this:

> We of the West were determined to establish a democratic government with as broad a base as possible and this made it easy to accept Communist participation in the Italian government. . . . Even if we had been contrarily disposed, it would have been difficult to deny Communist participation in the Italian government. Disciplined, militant Communist groups, particularly in the industrial areas of Northern Italy, had been the rallying point for Italian opposition to the Germans.

This policy may well have been a mistake — but it clearly was not "connived" at. And, far from crediting Stevenson with any role in our Italian policy, General Smith emphasized the role of General Eisenhower and of his political adviser, Robert Murphy, later the Deputy Under-Secretary of State in the Eisenhower administration.

The point is not merely that Senator McCarthy distorted the truth in three instances, nor even that he abused documents in doing so. The point is that, by weaving together false and distorted references and quotations, he ended up by presenting a totally false picture of Adlai Stevenson as a Communist. And this falsehood, combined with all the others, was intended to drive another nail into Stevenson' political coffin by the repeated insinuation of treason.

As McCarthy put it on an earlier occasion:

> We are finding proof, not of guilt by association, but of guilt by collaboration. . . . After your entire record is given them, and I can assure you it will be given before November 4, if the American people want you, they can have you. I don't think they will.

D. The Doctoring of Photographs

The doctoring of photographs is one aspect of the abuse of documents. On two occasions McCarthy staff members have engaged in this type of activity.

1. Browder-Tydings episode

In the 1950 Senatorial election campaign in Maryland, McCarthy made available to the anti-Tydings forces members of his staff, including Jean Kerr, his research assistant (the present Mrs.

McCarthy), and Don Surine. (The Senator himself was not active in the campaign.)

Prominent in this campaign was a four-page tabloid, *From the Record,* which was widely distributed in Maryland. This document featured a photograph of Tydings standing close to Earl Browder, the Communist leader — apparently engrossed in conversation with him.

The only thing wrong with this picture was that it was a fake. It was a composite picture, produced by the juxtaposition of two separate photographs.

A bipartisan Senate committee set up to investigate the Maryland election unanimously condemned the campaign conducted by McCarthy's staff. The election, reported the committee, "brought into sharp focus certain campaign tactics and practices that can be characterized as . . . destructive of fundamental American principles."

2. *The Schine-Stevens episode*

During the Army-McCarthy hearings, the McCarthy side tried to prove that Secretary Stevens, contrary to his testimony, had not always felt improperly pressured in behalf of Private G. David Schine. To back up this point the Senator introduced into the hearings a photograph of Schine and Stevens which had purportedly been made at Stevens' request.

The very next day it was demonstrated that the picture had been cropped to leave the misleading impression of Stevens and Schine alone together.

For the next three days, the subcommittee sought in vain to determine the responsibility for doctoring this picture. Finally, it put on the stand a member of the McCarthy staff, James Juliana, who conceded under oath that he had ordered the picture cropped.

While the committee sought the truth in this matter, Senator McCarthy remained silent about it.

E. *The "Letter" from J. Edgar Hoover*

As a final illustration of the Senator's abuse of documents, there is the famous "letter" he sought to introduce into the Army-McCarthy hearings with the claim that it was written by J. Edgar Hoover. McCarthy was seeking to invoke the name and authority of the FBI chief to bolster his claim of Communist espionage in the Army.

But this tactic backfired almost immediately. Hoover said he had never written such a letter. And the "document" was itself spurious — a partially accurate but unofficial summary of a much longer FBI report on the security situation at Fort Monmouth.

And so, in the Senator's arsenal of calculated deceit, the abuse of documents takes a prominent position.

III. INSINUATION AND INNUENDO

Insinuation: The deliberate imputation of unfavorable qualities to another man. In this context, the implication that a man is a Communist and a traitor.

Innuendo: The careful dropping of a hint, generally by indirection, to bolster the insinuation.

Here are a few examples of the Senator's resort to this technique.

A. *Adlai Stevenson*

In the now-famous "slip of the tongue" in the television speech against Stevenson, McCarthy said: "Alger — I mean Adlai." This innuendo, with its introduction of the first name of Hiss, needs no comment.

In another speech during the same campaign, the Senator assured an audience that if he could board the Stevenson campaign train with a "slippery-elm club" he could make a "good American" out of Stevenson — the insinuation being that Stevenson is not a good American.

B. *Nathan Pusey*

A favorite technique of the Senator is what might be called the "inverted" or "negative innuendo," which packs an even greater wallop because of its "inverted" nature.

In 1953, when Dr. Pusey became president of Harvard University, Senator McCarthy, a fellow-townsman from Appleton, Wisconsin, was asked to comment. He said: "I do not think Dr. Pusey is or has been a member of the Communist Party."

He could, of course, have said the same thing about the Pope or about the President of the United States. The effect of this seeming irrelevancy is precisely to raise the doubt that it appears to deny.

C. *Drew Pearson*

For several years the Senator has had a running feud with this commentator. One need not be a partisan of Pearson, on the score either of his reportorial reliability or of his political record, to recognize the intention of the Senator's "negative innuendo" when he told the Senate in December 1950: "It appears that Pearson never actually signed up as a member of the Communist Party and never paid dues. . . ."

D. Commonweal

Senator McCarthy also used innuendo in his attack on the Catholic weekly *The Commonweal*. In an interview in August 1953, McCarthy said: "I never said *The Commonweal* was Communist. I just said that, in front of the Jenner Committee [Senate Internal Security Subcommittee], one of its writers refused to say whether he is a Communist or not. From that you can draw your own conclusions."

The Commonweal wrote to McCarthy with the request that he identify the writer he referred to. In his reply the Senator asked the editors "what connection Thomas Davin has with *The Commonweal* — whether he writes for it, whether he has any voice in determination of policy, etc."

The periodical subsequently reported:

We . . . assured Senator McCarthy that Mr. Davin had never at any time written a single line for *The Commonweal,* that he has never had the slightest voice in determining the magazine's policy, and that previous to the present incident, four of the present five editors had never heard of him.

We therefore ask the Senator to make a public correction of his own statement (with its dark innuendo: "from that you can draw your own conclusions.").

The Senator never replied or retracted.

E. President Eisenhower

This final example of insinuation is perhaps the most striking.

At a critical point in the McCarthy-Army hearings the Senator sought to elicit testimony from several Presidential aides about a meeting they had held to discuss the Army's troubled relations with the Senator. President Eisenhower issued an order prohibiting such testimony on constitutional grounds.

The Senator immediately accused the President of dropping an "Iron Curtain" around the truth. The Administration, he charged, was hiding behind "a kind of Fifth Amendment."

The Senator's deliberate use of "Iron Curtain" and "Fifth Amendment" — terms generally associated with Communism — allowed of only one unmistakable interpretation: McCarthy was insinuating that the tactics of the Republican administration paralleled those of the Communists in the Soviet Union and in the United States.

IV.   THE SLANDER AMALGAM

The slander amalgam. This tactic has two elements: (a) The slurring of necessary distinctions between undercover Communist espionage agents, Party members subject to Party discipline, fellow-travelers who are consistent followers of the Party line and who may be Party instruments, and innocent dupes who foolishly permitted their names to be used by Communist-front organizations. (b) The mounting of an attack on an opponent or a critic by sandwiching him in with these types.

A.   Adlai Stevenson

Senator McCarthy, in his pre-election attack on the Democratic candidate, linked the name of Adlai Stevenson with those of Alger Hiss, a convicted traitor; Frank Coe, accused as a Communist; and the Communist-lining Institute of Pacific Relations. This is slander by amalgam.

B.   Newspapers and Magazines

Another example may be seen in the Senator's repeated attacks on newspapers that criticize him. Thus he refers to the New York *Post* as the "uptown edition of the *Daily Worker*," to the Washington *Post* as the "local edition," to the Milwaukee *Journal* as the "Milwaukee edition," and so on. He has said that *Time* and the *Saturday Evening Post* follow the Communist line as "laid down by the National Conference of the Communist Party."

C.   Edward R. Murrow

The most striking instance of the Senator's use of the slander amalgam was his attack on Edward R. Murrow. In April 1954 the commentator had devoted one session of his Columbia Broadcasting System television program "See It Now" to an examination of McCarthy in action.

The Senator replied in a telecast on time made available by Murrow:

... Murrow is a symbol, the leader and the cleverest of the jackal pack which is always found at the throat of anyone who dares to expose individual Communists and traitors.

I am compelled by the facts to say to you that Mr. Edward R. Murrow, as far back as twenty years ago, was engaged in propaganda for Communist causes. For example, the Institute of International Education, of which he was Acting Director, was chosen to act as a representative by a Soviet agency to do a job which would normally be done by the Russian Secret Police.

Mr. Murrow sponsored a Communist school in Moscow. In the selection of American students and teachers who were to attend, Murrow's organization acted for the Russion espionage and propaganda organization known as VOKS. ... Murrow's organization selected such notorious Communists as Isadore Bugin and David Zablodowsky. ...

Now Mr. Murrow by his own admission was a member of the IWW ... Murrow ... followed implicitly the Communist line as laid down in the last six months, laid down not only by the Communist *Daily Worker* but by the Communist magazine *Political Affairs*, and by the National Conference of the Communist Party. ...

Now, as you know, Owen Lattimore has been named as a conscious, articulate instrument of the Communist conspiracy. With respect to testimony in regard to his Communist activities, in his book *Ordeal by Slander*, he says: "I owe a very special debt to men I have never met. I must mention at least Edward R. Murrow."

Then there is the book by Harold Laski, admittedly the greatest Communist propagandist of our time in England. In his book *Reflections on the Revolution of Our Time*, he dedicates the book, "To my friends, E. R. Murrow and Lanham Tichener, with affection." ...

To this cause [of exposing Communists] ... I have dedicated all that I have and all that I am, and I want to assure you that I will not be deterred by the attacks of the Murrows, the Lattimores, the Fosters, the *Daily Worker*, or the Communist Party itself.

Here is the slander amalgam at its most effective — Murrow being connected with the Russian secret police, with a Soviet espionage agency, with known Communists, with Owen Lattimore, with the Communist Party and its press, with the Industrial Workers of the World (an old-time anarchist organization), and with William Z. Foster (head of the American Communist Party).

These are the facts:

(1) Murrow was never engaged in Communist propaganda. The Institute for International Education, of which he was assistant director from 1932 to 1935, was and is the American clearing-house for government and private student-exchange programs. Among its many distinguished trustees has been John Foster Dulles.

In 1934 the Institute sponsored a summer session for American students at Moscow University — as well as at other schools in England, France, and Germany. (This was a year after the United States recognized the Soviet Union.) VOKS, the Soviet bureau in charge of such matters, took care of travel arrangements and living facilities.

But after that single session the Soviets refused to have anything more to do with the Institute. After World War II the Communists branded the Institute as "the center of international propaganda for American reaction."

(2) Murrow, according to McCarthy, "by his own admission was a member of the IWW." Murrow has denied any such affiliation.

(3) Harold Laski was not "admittedly the greatest Communist propagandist of our time in England." Laski was not a Communist. He was a leading member of the British Labor Party, and one of its foremost ideologists, although his ideas were rarely accepted by the Labor Party. Laski was a fairly consistent apologist for the Soviet Union — and at the same time a vigorous opponent of the British Communist Party. (He was altogether somewhat erratic.)

His dedication of a book to Murrow was, as he made clear, based on his admiration for Murrow's World War II broadcasts.

(4) The connection between Murrow and Lattimore is even more tenuous. As Lattimore stated, he did not even know Murrow personally. Lattimore may have felt he owed a debt to the commentator because, in his reporting of the McCarran committee hearings, Murrow had defended Lattimore. But this does not make Murrow a Communist-sympathizer — as McCarthy insinuated.

V.   INTIMIDATION

Intimidation: To frighten or pressure an opponent by threatening his security or his public reputation.

Senator McCarthy has achieved much of his power by intimidation. Politicians have hesitated to offend him lest they become victims of his blistering attacks. Government employees, no matter how loyal, do not relish the prospect of investigation by the Senator.

A few outstanding examples of the Senator's use of this tactic will supply a clear operational definition of it.

A. Drew Pearson

Ordinarily Senator McCarthy does not resort to physical violence. But in December 1950 he picked a fight with Drew Pearson in Washington, with inconclusive results.

McCarthy subsequently attacked Pearson in a speech on the Senate floor, urging the public to boycott the commentator's radio sponsor, the Adam Hat Company. Shortly thereafter the company withdrew its sponsorship of the Pearson program (but denied it had acted in response to McCarthy's pressure).

B. Time

The Senator used the boycott gambit on other occasions. In 1951 *Time* ran an article critical of McCarthy. The Senator thereupon charged *Time* with obstructing the fight against Communists. And he appealed to the magazine's advertisers to withdraw their patronage. *Time* survived the attack.

C. Milwaukee Journal

In August 1951 McCarthy responded to criticism in the Milwaukee *Journal* by urging Wisconsin advertisers to withdraw their patronage from that newspaper. Said the Senator: "Keep in mind when you send your checks over to the *Journal* or pay a nickel a piece, you are contributing to bringing the Communist Party line into the homes of Wisconsin." The *Journal* survived the attack.

D. New York Post

In May 1953, as we have noted, the Senator conducted an inquiry into the editorial policy and personnel make-up of the New York *Post,* edited by James Wechsler. Wechsler was not intimidated — but a less courageous editor might have been. In any event, the Senator's investigation of the *Post* was widely recognized as attempted intimidation of a newspaper critical of him.

VI. ATTRIBUTING SIGNIFICANCE TO THE IRRELEVANT

Attributing significance to the irrelevant: Drawing conclusions from facts that are not pertinent.

The most enlightening illustration of the use of this technique was provided by the Senator's investigation of the United States information program. As shown in Chapter 2 above, this investigation — characterized by Counsel Roy Cohn as McCarthy's most important work in 1953 — consisted of the elicitation of a long series of non-pertinent facts, which the Senator sought to puff up to the proportions of organized subversion.

Without in any instance adducing evidence of either sinister motivations or subversive results, the Senator based his case on utter irrelevancies:

(1) The decision to cancel Hebrew broadcasts — clearly the result of both budgetary and propaganda considerations — became, in McCarthy's version, a deliberate attempt to deprive the United States of a great propaganda weapon. (See Chapter 2.)

(2) In the case of "Baker West," what was at worst a technical engineering mistake — and perhaps not a mistake at all — became, in McCarthy's version, a subversive attempt to cripple the Voice of America's message of freedom to the Soviet world. (See Chapter 2.)

(3) The youthful indiscretions of Theodore Kaghan — one of this country's chief anti-Communist propagandists in Germany — were transformed, in the Senator's hands, into a sinister pattern of subversion, to the utter disregard of the man's effective anti-Communist fight in the crucial years of the Cold War. (See Chapters 2 and 4.)

VII.   THE BLUFF AND THE DIVERSIONARY GAMBIT

Bluff: A big threat, followed by silence or evasion.
Diversionary gambit: A variant of the bluff; the hit-and-run tactic; *or,* the refusal to meet criticism directly; turning criticism aside by issuing counter-charges.

A.   Attacks on the Administration

As summarized in the last section of the preceding chapter, the Senator's record during the first year and one-half of the Republican administration was characterized by the hit-and-run technique. When defeated or stymied in a given situation, he changed his tack and veered in a different direction, rarely conceding defeat or error, always hiding behind a new offensive.

B.   John F. Floberg

One of the obscure phases of Senator McCarthy's career has to do with his service in the Marine Corps and the circumstances that led the Navy to award to him in 1952 — somewhat belatedly — the Distinguished Flying Cross and the Air Medal with four stars. The awards were approved by Assistant Secretary of the Navy John F. Floberg.

Apparently concerned lest Floberg, who was being questioned by newsmen, disclose uncomfortable items in his war record, McCarthy wrote the Secretary a peremptory letter in an attempt to insure Floberg's silence. McCarthy wrote he had heard Floberg was "displaying classified material" and he ordered him "to prepare a report to me on such activities on your part and have it available for presentation to me as Chairman of the Senate Investigating Committee."

Floberg coolly ignored the order, replying merely that he had not at any time disclosed classified material to any unauthorized person. McCarthy never renewed the demand.

C. The Benton Libel Suit

In September 1951 Senator Benton, outside of his Senatorial immunity, made ten charges of misconduct by Senator McCarthy. Facing re-election, McCarthy filed a $2,000,000 libel suit against Benton. Three years later, in March 1954, McCarthy dropped the suit (legally committing himself never to reopen it) on the pretext that his lawyers had been unable to discover a single person in the whole United States who believed any of Benton's charges.

McCarthy's bluff was promptly called by hundreds of people who announced publicly their willingness to testify that they believed Benton's charges against McCarthy.

D. The Hornell Hart Study

In 1951 Professor Hornell Hart of Duke University prepared a study entitled *McCarthy Versus the State Department*. Dr. Hart submitted the manuscript to all persons mentioned in the study, including the Senator, with a request for comments and suggestions.

Two McCarthy staff members, Jean Kerr and Don Surine, wrote the professor a series of letters denouncing the study. Then the Senator himself wrote to the president of Duke University, threatening a libel suit:

> . . . this preliminary draft of the Hart report contains a vast amount of vicious, false and libellous attacks. . . . This is to notify you personally of Mr. Hart's project, in case you are not aware of it at this time, and that I shall hold the University legally accountable for the publication of this document.

Later the Senator repeated the threat of a libel suit.

After the appearance of the Hart report, the Senator remained silent. The bluff was called — and no libel suit ensued.

E. The Lehman Incident

In 1951, during one of his speeches on the Senate floor, McCarthy brandished a document which he alleged to be a letter written by Owen Lattimore to Joseph Barnes.[2] He invited skeptical colleagues to step across the aisle to his desk and examine it.

To his evident surprise, Senator Lehman accepted the offer. When Lehman approached McCarthy's desk, the Wisconsin Senator refused to show the letter. "I yield no further," he exclaimed.

F. The Appeal to the Lie Detector

The Senator's favorite diversionary gambit is the appeal to the lie detector. He has resorted to it on a number of occasions, at least two of which are notable:

1. The Malmédy Case

After failing (as we showed on page 62) to entrap his intended victim, Lieutenant Perl, the Senator called upon him to submit to a lie-detector test. This was a perfectly safe challenge. McCarthy knew that no Senate committee had ever used the lie detector and would not now use it. What Senator would relinquish his own judgment of truth and falsehood to the decision of a machine?

When the subcommittee refused to go along with him, McCarthy walked out dramatically, charging "whitewash."

2. The Bohlen Case

In 1953 the Senator made a similar grandstand play, this time on the floor of the Senate. Despite assurances from Senators Taft and Knowland that Bohlen's security status was above reproach, McCarthy demanded that Bohlen submit to a lie-detector test.

He knew this was an empty challenge. He knew the Senate would not approve his suggestion — especially since his demand meant a challenge of the veracity of his two Republican colleagues, Senators Knowland and Taft.

---

[2] Joseph Barnes, formerly an editor of the New York *Herald Tribune,* later an editor of the New York *Star,* is now with Simon & Schuster, publishers. Mr. Barnes, together with Lattimore, was charged by witnesses at the McCarran committee hearings with Communist activities.

VIII. THE PERSONAL SPY NETWORK

Personal spy network: The use by a politician of an apparatus of spies and informers loyal specifically to himself and operating independently of government security systems.

The employment by a United States Senator of a personal espionage organization — complete with paid investigators and all the technical apparatus of the trade — is something new in American history.

Senator McCarthy began building his network soon after his 1950 debut as an anti-Communist. Within a few months the professionals on his staff numbered nearly a score, including paid occasional and part-time agents and correspondents in this country and abroad.

A. Informants in the Executive Branch

Among the sensations produced by the McCarthy-Army hearings were McCarthy's admission that he received confidential information from people throughout the Executive Branch, and his open encouragement to all "2,000,000 Federal employees" to supply him with such material in the future.

B. "The Loyal American Underground"

The McCarthy investigation of the Voice of America revealed the deployment in force of a personal espionage apparatus known as the "Loyal American Underground." Its organizer and leader was reported to be Paul Deac, a disaffected member of the French Desk.

Deac's group became the semi-official witness-recruiting agency for the McCarthy subcommittee. Deac himself frequently served subpoenas on witnesses who were summoned to the subcommittee's unofficial headquarters in David Schine's suite at the Waldorf Towers. And there Deac and some of his cohorts functioned as unofficial major-domos. This "underground" evidently extended throughout the Voice and supplied the Senator with much of the material for his unfounded accusations.

C. The Stevenson Economic Report

The Stevenson economic report on Italy (see page 69) was declassified by the State Department two days after McCarthy referred to it. In his speech the Senator had appeared to be quoting it. But since his "quotations" were all askew, it cannot be stated with certainty that he actually possessed a copy of this confidential document.

If he did not, then this was just another bluff. If he did have it, the questions arise: How did he get it? What was his source?

D. The Hoover "Letter"

The Hoover "letter" received much attention during the Army-McCarthy hearings. The Senator identified his source as "a young Army officer in Intelligence," but he refused to reveal the identity of the lawbreaker.

There is no reason to doubt the Senator's word on his source: his private espionage network operates effectively through infiltration of many Executive departments, with his overt encouragement.

McCarthy's use of a personal spy network is directly related to his contempt for the law.

IX. CONTEMPT FOR THE LAW

Contempt for the Law: The attitude that self-interest justifies the defiance or evasion of the law.

Senator McCarthy's political career is studded with instances of a cavalier attitude toward the law. Only recently has he attempted to justify this contemptuous attitude — by an appeal to "a loyalty that towers over any Presidential order." On this basis he excuses and justifies (a) his encouragement of Federal employees to violate their oath of office; and (b) his own revelation of confidential documents.

But this cavalier attitude toward the law did not always find its higher sanction in the anti-Communist "crusade"; it appears as a black streak throughout the Senator's public career.

A. Wisconsin Circuit Judge McCarthy (1941)

As a circuit judge, McCarthy repeatedly postponed and finally dismissed an action brought by the Wisconsin state department of agriculture against a local dairy. When the department of agriculture appealed his decision to the state supreme court, it was discovered that, in dismissing the action, McCarthy had ordered the destruction of an important document.

The state supreme court declared that "this action constituted an abuse of judicial power."

B. *The Marine and the Tax Collector* (1944)

Judge McCarthy took a leave of absence from the bench in 1942 to serve a hitch as an intelligence officer with the Marine Corps in the South Pacific.

During this period he made over $40,000 in stock-market speculation. But he neglected to mention this fact in his 1943 income-tax return.

Several years later, when questioned by Internal Revenue officials, he avoided payment of taxes by claiming non-residence — since he had at the time been serving in the Pacific.

In 1944, however, while still in service, McCarthy was very eager to claim Wisconsin residence, in order to qualify as a candidate in the Republican Senatorial primary of that year.

C. *The Judge Campaigns for the Senate* (1946)

Although McCarthy's term as circuit judge was not to expire until 1951, he entered the Senatorial primary campaign in 1946. The Wisconsin constitution forbids a circuit judge to hold any other office, except a judicial one, during his term.

McCarthy's disregard of this constitutional provision led the state board of bar examiners to ask the Wisconsin supreme court to take disciplinary action against him. The court ruled that because McCarthy was running for a federal rather than a state office it had no jurisdiction. But it also declared that McCarthy, "by accepting and holding the office of U. S. Senator during the term for which he was elected Circuit Judge, did so in violation of the terms of the Constitution and the laws of the State of Wisconsin."

The details of this contempt for the law may change from year to year, according to the fashion of the season. But the basic attitude remains.

X. THE UNFOUNDED CHARGE OF TREASON

Treason: Giving aid and comfort to the enemies of one's country. In McCarthy's book: any serious opposition from any quarter.

The Senator's use of the charge — or the unmistakable insinuation — of treason conforms to an inner logic of its own. It follows a clear, dynamic principle which, if the Senator cannot be said to have discovered, he has applied more doggedly, more ferociously, and more effectively than any predecessor. This principle might be formulated as McCarthy's Law of Perpetual Expansion.

It is as though, through growing experience and knowledge, the Senator has discovered that the larger, the more general, the more preposterous the charge, the less open it is to rational examination — and consequently the more effective it is for its purpose.

This revelation evidently came upon the Senator in a series of stages.

A. The First Stage (1950)

Despite the sensation caused by McCarthy's opening salvo in 1950, his first charges encompassed only a relatively restricted area: he imputed treason only to members of the State Department.

B. The Second Stage (1951)

At this stage, the Senator pushed farther back in time and farther afield in space. He moved on from the Acheson State Department to General George Marshall and all the wartime and post-war policies Marshall represented.

C. The Third Stage (1952)

By the fall of that election year, the implication of treason was no longer limited to the genuine or imaginary sins of omission and commission of Acheson and Marshall and their regimes. It now extended to the wholly hallucinatory sins of Adlai Stevenson.

And that significant extension hinted, by its very nature, at the next stage, which flowered eighteen months later.

D. The Fourth Stage (1954)

On Lincoln's Birthday in 1954, four years to the day after McCarthy's arrival at the anti-Communist front, the Senator unveiled his charge of treason in full dimension. It was now to be "Twenty Years of Treason." This is how he put it:

> The issue between the Republicans and the Democrats is clearly drawn. It has been deliberately drawn by those who have been in charge of twenty years of treason. The hard fact is, the hard fact is that those who wear the label, those who wear the label Democrat, wear it with the stain of an historic betrayal.

> At least twenty million Americans are implicated by this charge of treason.

E.   *The Fifth Stage* (1954)

McCarthy's use of the charge of treason reached its climax when it was extended, on May 28, 1954, to encompass by implication President Eisenhower himself.

Eisenhower had already been implicated — indirectly and cautiously — during the earlier attack on General Marshall. For, as the Senator put it even then, in all of Marshall's "fatal" wartime policies, General Eisenhower was his faithful and loyal supporter.

But this innuendo was clarified to a considerable extent only when the issue between the Senator and the President was fully drawn during the Army-McCarthy hearings. In his attack on Attorney General Brownell's statement which reiterated, with the President's approval, the principle of the security of Executive Branch files, Senator McCarthy charged that such a policy of secrecy would hamper his investigation of traitorous activities in the government.

His exact phrase was: "treason during the last twenty or *twenty-one* years." (Italics added.)

In February 1954, it was still only "twenty years" of treason. By May, a brief three months later, it had been extended to "twenty-one years." This extension can only mean the encompassing of the present President of the United States.

Farther than this, higher than this, Senator McCarthy cannot go. And that is why McCarthy's whole charge of treason must inevitably fall of its own dead weight.

And, amidst all the sound and fury and hullabaloo of these charges, *real* traitors may be going unnoticed.

In the foregoing pages we have examined Senator McCarthy's use of ten methods in his political in-fighting: the multiple untruth, the abuse of documents, insinuation and innuendo, the slander amalgam, intimidation, attributing significance to the irrelevant, the bluff and the diversionary gambit, the personal spy network, contempt for the law, and the unfounded charge of treason.

The Senator maintains that he operates this way in order to further his "fight for America."

In the following pages we shall examine the effects and significance of this "fight." For we must determine whether this kind of fight is becoming to a free people.

4. The Results

> "A State which dwarfs its men, in order that they be more docile instruments in its hands even for beneficial purposes, will find that with small men no great thing can really be accomplished."
>
> JOHN STUART MILL

In November 1952 Father Leon Sullivan, a Catholic missionary who had been imprisoned by the Chinese Communists, wrote an article for the Catholic weekly *Commonweal*. He described his experiences under Communist imprisonment and his feelings on returning to freedom and to his native land. This is one of the things he had to say:

> I would rather return to my Chinese Communist prison cell than avail myself of Senator McCarthy's "protection." His is as great, if not a greater threat to American freedom than the military might of the Kremlin, and, believe me, I do not underestimate either the Kremlin's might or its cleverness.

Why did Father Sullivan write these words? What impelled this man, returning to America after years of service and sacrifice abroad, to utter these words of shock? What did he see here that led him to such an extreme exaggeration of the situation? What had Senator McCarthy wrought that led the priest to utter this stinging protest?

These are the chief results of Senator McCarthy's "crusade":

(I) He has seriously impaired the operation of Fort Monmouth, the nation's Number One research laboratory for defense against atomic attack.

(II) He has grievously disrupted the effectiveness of the Voice of America, the nation's chief anti-Communist propaganda arm.

(III) He has gravely threatened the integrity and usefulness of the Foreign Service, the nation's eyes and ears abroad.

86

(IV) He has wantonly injured the processes of constitutional government by stimulating and exploiting a network of private informers throughout the government.

(V) He has spread disunity at home by attempting to undermine the nation's confidence in its highest civilian and military leaders, and by imputing disloyal motives to innocent citizens.

(VI) He has spread disunity in the free world by symbolizing fanatical forces of unreason which free men abroad fear may be taking over America. In doing so, he has played directly into the hands of the Communists, whose major aim is to drive a wedge between the United States and its allies and friends abroad.

Beyond all of these specific effects (which we shall discuss in this chapter), McCarthy has come to represent a spirit which is inherent in all of his own activities and which threatens to spread, if it is not checked, into many other realms of our public life. This spirit is characterized by:

(1) *Contempt for the intellectual life* without which a nation is powerless to plan its welfare and its defense.

(2) *The creation of a climate of uncertainty among the nation's civil servants* whose untroubled functioning is indispensable to the process of government.

(3) *The stimulation of a narrow, restrictive standard of internal security* which threatens to slow down and perhaps ultimately to paralyze effective government by making it impossible for men of proven loyalty and tried ability to serve the nation.

(4) *The encouragement of an unhealthy note of caution* which many unnecessarily frightened people in and out of government have allowed to pervade their thought and limit their expression.

Let us examine the impact of Senator McCarthy's activities, case by case.

I. THE IMPAIRMENT OF FORT MONMOUTH

Walter Millis, distinguished military analyst of the New York *Herald Tribune,* in these words summed up the impact of Senator McCarthy on the nation's research laboratory for defense against atomic attack:

This really vital and sensitive military installation has been wrecked — more thoroughly than any Soviet saboteur could have dreamed of doing it — by the kind of anti-Communism of which Senator McCarthy has made himself the leader.

The Fort Monmouth situation is truly scandalous. It is so scandalous that some who have looked into it, thoroughly conservative in outlook and Republican in politics, are talking about demanding a Congressional investigation . . . into the processes of witchhunting, bigotry, cowardice, race prejudice, and sheer incompetence which have turned one of our top-level military-scientific operations into a mare's nest of exasperation, fear, and futility. . . .

The personal injustice involved is not here considered. The impairment of the national defense is something which no one whose life may one day hang upon the excellence of our radar screens can dare to disregard.

A. Disruption of the Operation

(1) The scientists and technicians implicated in the course of the McCarthy investigation are mostly on the higher civil-service level. They have an average of twenty-five to thirty productive years remaining before retirement.

This means, in the case of those not restored to their jobs, that a large number of highly skilled man-years will be lost to the government.

(2) While these men are not indispensable or irreplaceable, it is estimated that they could not be adequately replaced in less than a year.

This means that their projects will be seriously handicapped in the meantime.

(3) In the most important of the scientific laboratories at Monmouth, Evans Laboratory, 7 out of 29 section chiefs have been removed from their jobs. As a result roughly 15 per cent of all laboratory personnel at Monmouth lost their supervisory guidance. And in many cases the persons removed were considered essential to their projects.

All of this means that a great many vital defense projects of this nation have been disrupted or seriously crippled, with the resultant waste of many millions of taxpayers' dollars.

B. Damage to Morale

(1) Morale at Monmouth has been seriously damaged. This demoralization is not restricted to employees involved in the investigation. It has spread through the ranks of the vast majority who have not been personally involved.

The combination of demoralization in the ranks with the removal of highly skilled, responsible scientific leaders is thus a further contribution to the disruption of the operation.

(2) The sensational publicity given to the case by Senator Mc-Carthy's briefings to the press contributed largely to the demoralization. It was not made clear for a long time, either publicly or within Monmouth, that the McCarthy witnesses who invoked the Fifth Amendment were *not* connected with Monmouth, that all Monmouth employees vigorously denied charges of Communist affiliation or association, and that they did *not* take refuge behind the Fifth Amendment.

Thus the implicated employees suffered hardship and undeserved prejudice among their fellow-employees and in the community.

But even the non-implicated employees were adversely affected by the unjustified but widely accepted impression of large-scale disloyalty at Monmouth.

(3) Many Monmouth scientists, not themselves implicated, are preparing to leave government employ at some future time when it will not reflect on their loyalty or security status.

This trend will contribute to the further disruption of the operation.

(4) Finally scientists have raised a serious question vitally affecting public policy: Will the public sensations raised by Senator McCarthy, and the resultant demoralization, have a deleterious effect on the future recruitment of much-needed scientific personnel for government defense work?

C. The Establishment of Self-defeating Security Standards

Another equally damaging and possibly more dangerous result of the McCarthy impact on Monmouth was the introduction of petty, restrictive, and self-defeating security practices.

It seems clear that the Army action, spurred on by the intrusion of Senator McCarthy, was precipitate, unfair, indecisive, and confusing. Security officers at Monmouth seemed to have no firm set of guiding principles in evaluating the raw data about employees. They seemed to be unaware of any real basis on which to judge security risks.

This is apparent from the large number of trivial charges leveled against the implicated employees. For example:

(1) One man is accused of favoring the views of Max Lerner. Lerner is a professor and newspaper columnist who holds and expresses views on a wide variety of subjects, political and non-political alike. He is and always has been a liberal. Like many liberals during the Popular Front period of the 1930's and the Grand Alliance period of the 1940's, Lerner was too often duped

by the Communist Party line. But he was never a Communist, and since 1948 his position has been clearly anti-Communist. (In that year he urged the Democratic Party to nominate Dwight D. Eisenhower as its candidate for President.)

(2) Another man is charged with considering the possibility of sending a copy of a technical article he had published in a scientific magazine to a scientist in Czechoslovakia who had requested it. Actually the employee never sent the article. Furthermore the magazine in which his article had appeared has worldwide circulation and is available behind the Iron Curtain. Finally, the employee did not even consider sending the article. What he actually did was to report the request to the security officer and discuss it with him.

The lack of intelligent standards for judging security is also reflected in the fluctuations between suspension, declassification, and clearance to which many of the employees have been subjected. In one case an individual found himself in all three categories during the course of the investigation. In another case, an individual's clearance to handle classified material was lifted and he was later called before the McCarthy committee — all as a result of mistaken identity.

Such mistakes and lack of standards raise the question of whether security officers are always competent to discern real threats to national security, whether the haphazard standards and procedures they apparently feel themselves forced to adopt do not result in the defeat of their very purposes.

The impact of Senator McCarthy on Fort Monmouth exhibits all the characteristic features of the spirit he represents: contempt for the intellectual life, the creation of a climate of uncertainty among the nation's civil servants, the stimulation of a narrow, restrictive standard of internal security, and the encouragement of an unhealthy note of caution.

II. THE DISRUPTION OF THE VOICE OF AMERICA

Dr. Robert L. Johnson, president of Temple University, in February 1953 was appointed by President Eisenhower to be the new head of the International Information Administration. In July 1953 he resigned because of ill health. At that time he issued a statement and a letter to Senator McCarthy, in which he said:

The reputation of the American people has suffered enough as a result of irresponsible charges and actions in connection with our program abroad. The only group that has gained through these wicked attacks has been the Communist international movement. It is one of the tragic ironies of our time that some of those "who are in the forefront of the fight against Communism" are among those who are damaging the action programs that do battle against it.

In those few sentences, Dr. Johnson summed up the impact of Senator McCarthy on the information program.

How did it happen?

A. Damage to the Operation

As the weeks of the McCarthy investigation went by, it became clear that the State Department not only was bowing to the Senator's wishes but was going far beyond what even he seemed to demand — an unmistakable token of his devastating impact on frightened officials. For instance:

(1) When Senator McCarthy charged that the alleged mislocation of the two powerful transmitters was doing the work of Stalin, the State Department canceled all construction on the project. But it went much further: Construction was never resumed even at presumably better locations.

(2) After McCarthy had finished his investigation of the Voice of America, the administration did not dare to ask for the kind of budget it would have wanted for this powerful anti-Communist instrument. The administration knew it would have a difficult time trying to get even a considerably reduced budget approved by a Congress "shocked" by the Senator's "revelations."

(3) It is impossible to gauge the exact loss caused to the program by the elimination of such distinguished public servants as Reed Harris and Theodore Kaghan, McCarthy's favorite targets. But loss there clearly was. During the months following the State Department's capitulation to McCarthy's onslaught, several first-rate propagandists left government service in order to take their talents to better-paying jobs in business or elsewhere. Similarly skilled replacements were not forthcoming as late as a year and a half after the Senator's visitation.

(4) The information program sustained a serious loss in the ultimate departure of Bertram Wolfe, an eminent anti-Communist propagandist and scholar. Wolfe was never in McCarthy's direct line of fire, although he was grazed by a ricochet.[1] He resigned because the restrictive atmosphere at the Voice of America, com-

[1] See page 27.

pounded of weak, small-minded leadership and excessive bureaucratic timidity, made it increasingly difficult for him to continue
the effective anti-Communist job he had joined the Voice to do.
Senator McCarthy had no small share in creating that restrictive
atmosphere.

B. Damage to Morale

The demoralization of Voice of America personnel was no
small accomplishment of the McCarthy investigation. Every concession made by the State Department was interpreted by many
of its employees as craven flight in the face of unwarranted accusations. The feeling spread that the Department would do nothing
to defend the integrity of any man so unfortunate as to come under
McCarthy's attack. This feeling of isolation was only aggravated
when Harris and Kaghan went down fighting, alone — and to the
accompaniment of official silence.

Every employee felt somehow involved, personally implicated.
This sense of personal involvement, even for the people who were
in no way under attack, was heightened by the morbid fascination
of the scenes on the television screen. Here, for all the world to
see, personal friends were branded as pro-Communists by fellow-
employees.

The uneasy position of Voice of America employees or former
employees was intensified when they had to face neighbors, friends,
and prospective employers after the McCarthy television proceedings. They were placed in the impossible position of defending,
clarifying, explaining away — and never perhaps quite dispelling
the last lingering doubts.

C. The Restrictive Security Standard — and Its Aftermath

1. The policy directives

For a period of six months, from February to July of 1953,
the United States presented to the world the curious spectacle of
waging anti-Communist psychological warfare by restricting the
freedom of expression and operation of its anti-Communist propaganda agency.

As mentioned above, on February 18, 1953, the day after the
International Information Administration hearings opened, Senator
McCarthy made clear his distinct displeasure with the original
policy directive allowing the selective use of Communist material in
anti-Communist propaganda warfare. The directive was immediately revoked.

During the first week in March the information agency issued a further directive specifying that no Communist material of any sort would be used under any circumstances unless it had previously been used by a reputable American source. This directive produced the crowning irony that the Voice of America had to seek special authorization to evade it in order to report and comment on the death of Stalin a few days later.

On March 17 the State Department ordered the information agency to withdraw from the overseas libraries any issues of responsible American periodicals that contained "material hostile to U.S. objectives." There was no hint as to the criteria by which to determine what might now be considered "hostile" — or who was to establish the criteria.

In June, Secretary of State Dulles told a news conference that a number of books in American overseas libraries had actually been burned. This was shortly after President Eisenhower had exhorted a Dartmouth College audience not to join the "book-burners." For Europeans this admission conjured up only one thought — the memory of Nazi book-burning. Meanwhile some overseas libraries had already been emasculated of anything remotely relating to controversial material. And, at the Voice of America headquarters in New York, the works of Harry Overstreet and Gilbert Highet could not be used for projected cultural programs because their "security status" was in question.

This extreme dénouement of the flight from sanity was officially reversed in July 1953. But much irreparable damage had already been done at home and abroad to the effectiveness and credibility of our anti-Communist message of freedom.

2. The case of Theodore Kaghan

What was remarkable in Kaghan's case was not so much that he was a target for Senator McCarthy as that McCarthy's attack induced the State Department to force Kaghan's resignation.[2]

Here was a man who had done yeoman work in the anti-Communist fight at the front line in Berlin. He had received encomiums from the highest European anti-Communist sources. Yet, when he returned to Washington to face the McCarthy committee, he received a cold shoulder at the State Department.

[2] Unquestionably, the State Department was embarrassed by Kaghan's characterization of Messrs. Cohn and Shine as "junketeering gumshoes" — they were after all official representatives of a Congressional investigating committee. Ordinarily, however, such an indiscretion would have drawn no more than an official rebuke.

And while his hearing was still in progress, he was informed that Scott McLeod, the departmental security officer, had asked for his resignation — or else McLeod would bring security charges against Kaghan. Not new charges, but the old ones which Kaghan had long since exploded. Bewildered, faced with what he considered treachery and cowardice where he had expected courage and integrity, Kaghan resigned.

After a farewell party for Kaghan in Bonn, following his return from Washington — a party attended by all the "brass" of HICOG including Dr. Conant — some of the guests were asked to supply a list of names of the other guests. Security officers were "just checking."

The impact of Senator McCarthy on the information program exhibits characteristic features of the spirit he represents: the establishment of a spirit of uncertainty and insecurity among civil servants, the new restrictive standard of internal security.

That was how the Senator grievously disrupted the effectiveness of the nation's chief anti-Communist propaganda arm.

III. THE THREAT TO THE FOREIGN SERVICE

On January 17, 1954, a letter from five distinguished retired diplomats[3] appeared in the New York *Times,* defining the nature of the threat Senator McCarthy has posed to the Foreign Service (without, however, mentioning the Senator by name).

They noted that the Foreign Service is, in effect, one of America's first lines of defense. Especially under present international circumstances, our diplomats are not striped-pants pencil-pushers. They are the authentic spokesmen abroad for America's policies and position. And, even more, they are the eyes and ears of America abroad. Their objective reporting and analysis constitute a good part of this country's intelligence work. And on them depends the construction of effective counter-intelligence work as well as an informed and effective foreign policy.

This crucial activity, in the opinion of the five former diplomats, is being crippled by the "emotional climate at home."

Foreign Service personnel have been subjected to a series of attacks on their loyalty and moral standards. With rare exceptions,

---

[3] Norman Armour, former Ambassador and Assistant Secretary of State; Robert Woods Bliss, former Ambassador to the Argentine; Joseph C. Grew, former Ambassador to Japan and Under-Secretary of State; William Phillips, former Ambassador and Under-Secretary of State; and G. Howland Shaw, former chief of the State Department's Near Eastern division.

these attacks have been based on little or no evidence; but the very repetition of accusations has served to reinforce their public acceptance. This has had some harmful results, in the view of these distinguished ex-diplomats:

> . . . a Foreign Service officer who reports on persons and events to the very best of his ability, and who makes recommendations which at the time he conscientiously believes to be in the interest of the United States, may subsequently find his loyalty and integrity challenged and may even be forced out of the service and discredited forever as a private citizen after many years of distinguished service. A premium therefore has been put upon reporting and upon recommendations which are ambiguously stated or so cautiously set forth as to be deceiving.
> When any such tendency begins its insidious work, it is not long before accuracy and initiative have been sacrificed to acceptability and conformity. The ultimate result is a threat to national security.

Exaggerated security procedures — administered by men imbued with narrow-minded, illiberal views and uninstructed as to the necessary balance between security and liberty in a democracy — have led to excesses which, if not checked, may threaten the very basis of successful Foreign Service operation. The most casual associations or innocent deviations from the norms of Babbittry among both candidates and career men become suspect.

Already a drop of 50 per cent in applications for the Foreign Service during 1953 has deprived the government of potentially valuable resources.

The effects of the spirit represented by Senator McCarthy can be devastating to this "first line of defense." This spirit can lead the state (in the words of John Stuart Mill) to "dwarf its men." Or, as Grew, Armour, and their associates put it: ". . . it is relevant to inquire whether we are not laying the foundations of a Foreign Service competent to serve a totalitarian government rather than the Government of the United States as we have heretofore known it."

It was not hysterical, fuzzy-minded liberals who put their names to this document; it was not "leftists" who expressed these fears. These men are sober, conservative, trained to caution in judgment and expression, who have rendered their country great service in the past thirty years.

Indeed, there is a crowning irony in the presence of Joseph Grew in this group. Clearly without his consent, he has been adopted by the forces that Senator McCarthy leads and represents, and has become an official part of their martyrology. Joseph Grew, former Under-Secretary of State and Ambassador to Japan under President Roosevelt, was, according to the McCarthyite version of history, eased out of the Department of State because of his staunch anti-Communism and his opposition to Acheson's "pro-Communist" dispositions within the Department.

It is this anti-Communist hero of the McCarthy forces who speaks out so strongly against the very spirit they have fostered.

Once again, the impact of Senator McCarthy on the Foreign Service exhibits characteristic features of the spirit he represents: the creation of a spirit of uncertainty and insecurity among civil servants, the stimulation of a new restrictive standard of internal security, the spread of an unhealthy note of caution in regard to both expression and activity.[4]

That was how Senator McCarthy gravely threatened the integrity and usefulness of one of the nation's first lines of defense.

IV. THE "AMERICAN UNDERGROUND" OF SPIES AND INFORMERS

On May 5, 1954, Senator McCarthy made an astonishing admission to his colleagues and the country. It occurred in a colloquy between himself and Senator Everett M. Dirksen during the Senate investigation of McCarthy's dispute with the Army. The subject under discussion was the confidential summary of a secret FBI security report — a report that had secretly been transmitted to Senator McCarthy in an unauthorized way, and by an Army officer unauthorized to do so.

SENATOR DIRKSEN. Senator McCarthy, is it unusual or extraordinary for confidential documents of this nature to come to you either as chairman of the Senate Permanent Investigating Committee or as an individual Senator?

SENATOR McCARTHY. It's a daily and a nightly occurrence for me to receive information from people in Government in regard to Communist infiltration.

SENATOR DIRKSEN. And that's true of many agencies in Government?

SENATOR McCARTHY. That is true. Very true.

[4] Reports indicate that at least some Foreign Service officers are now afraid to gain the confidence of intelligence sources close to foreign Communist functionaries because their contact with such persons — even in the official interest of U.S. intelligence services — may be held against them at some future date. What a masterstroke this has been for Communist underground movements in friendly countries!

This boast, given as sworn testimony, is striking evidence of the existence of an "American underground" in the government, a network of private informers who, despite the spirit of the law (if not of the law itself) and of constitutional processes of government, supply the Senator with confidential information to use as he sees fit. It is a network which McCarthy stimulates and exploits — and which he has, indeed, taken under his "protection."

In the ensuing colloquy between Army Counsel Joseph Welch and Senator McCarthy, Welch tried to get the Senator to give the committee the name of the Army officer who had broken the law in order to give him the confidential document. This was the reply:

SENATOR McCARTHY. Mr. Welch, I think I made it very clear to you that neither you nor anyone else will ever get me to violate the confidence of loyal people in this government who give me information about Communist infiltration. I repeat, you will not get their names, you will not get any information which will allow you to identify them. . . . You can go right ahead and try until doomsday. You will not get the names of any informants who rely upon me to protect them.

The phrase "American underground" is used advisedly. There actually was an organization by that name at the Voice of America. It was shrewdly led and well organized, extending into virtually every office of the Voice.[5]

It was this group that supplied McCarthy with much of the distorted information — the copies of confidential memoranda, the scripts quoted out of context, the tales of inter- and intra-office squabbles, the false and misleading reports of conversations — that he built up into his sensational, televised "case" against the Voice of America. This underground network did not restrict its activities to covering the persons and events that were ultimately implicated in the McCarthy hearings. It kept tabs on virtually every employee of the Voice — on his loyalty, efficiency, and moral standards. In the summer of 1954 some of Senator McCarthy's agents — whose names are known — were still employed at the Voice of America.

There may not be an actual organization of this type functioning in other agencies of the government. But there can be no doubt, as the Senator himself boasted, that he has a private army of informers strategically placed in many departments of government. This helps to explain some interesting points:

(1) How did McCarthy learn, in the fall of 1953, that the Army had instituted a secret security check of employees at Fort Monmouth?

[5] See page 81 above.

(2) How did McCarthy learn the contents of a confidential memorandum submitted by Monmouth's commanding general to Army Secretary Stevens?

(3) How did he obtain a report on a whole series of confidential memoranda from J. Edgar Hoover to the Secretary of the Army in 1951, 1952, and 1953?

(4) How did he know of the difference of opinion between Secretary Dulles and Scott McLeod on the Bohlen case?

These are just a few of the many questions which the existence of an "American underground" explains.

This fostering of a "government within a government" by Senator McCarthy

> — encourages the breaking of the law through the unauthorized disclosure of government secrets to unauthorized persons;
>
> — disrupts the orderly processes of government by breaking down the constitutional separation of powers and prerogatives of the Executive and Legislative branches;
>
> — damages morale by raising the specter of mutual suspicion and distrust among employees who can never be sure which of their colleagues is an informer and a tale-bearer;
>
> — impairs the principle of responsibility in government by encouraging subordinates to disregard the authority and leadership of their superiors and take their grievances to an external authority;
>
> —destroys the democratic understanding of the means-ends relationship through the immoral justification of lawlessness in the name of a higher end.

This is the very essence of disloyalty — to justify the breaking of the law and the violation of an oath of loyalty in public office on the basis of private convictions and views.

V. THE SPREADING OF DISUNITY AT HOME

Senator McCarthy has spread disunity at home — by his tactics of name-calling, by maligning a host of innocent citizens, by attempting to undermine the nation's confidence in its highest civilian and military leaders.

The Senator has often pleaded with his opponents to name one

— "just one" — case of an innocent person whom he has smeared or harmed. For some unaccountable reason those to whom this rhetorical question has been addressed have, on the record, failed to supply an answer. But Buckley and Bozell, the neophyte sophisticated intellectual apologists for the Senator, *have* supplied an answer — indeed several. They are forced to concede that McCarthy unjustly attacked Drew Pearson, Haldore Hanson, Dorothy Kenyon, Philip Jessup, and General George C. Marshall.

The Senator has argued that his attacks on General Marshall have failed to damage the General's reputation. This is a questionable assertion at best. It is known that President Eisenhower has always revered and admired General Marshall, and in the normal course of events he could have been expected to draw upon the General's wisdom and experience. That he has not done so — that, in fact, it would be politically embarrassing for him to do so — would seem to be the result, at least in part, of the Senator's assaults on General Marshall's loyalty and integrity.

However, the question as to whether the man was harmed is irrelevant compared with the vital question: What was McCarthy's intent? The list of his victims, intended and actual, is indeed long — and revealing.

It reveals, for example, that the Senator is unconcerned with whether these people are Communists or anti-Communists.

It reveals that he does not concern himself with their political affiliations and leanings: they may be Republicans or Democrats, liberals or conservatives.

All these people have been subjected to his spray-gun assaults. And this has not failed to foster disunity and passion.

McCarthy has of course devoted considerable effort to attacking his liberal opponents. In the summer and autumn of 1952 he concentrated on Adlai Stevenson ("Alger . . . I mean Adlai") and his liberal supporters, among them such distinguished anti-Communists as Arthur Schlesinger, Jr., James Wechsler, Bernard DeVoto, Wilson Wyatt, and Elmer Davis. Whether or not these men were hurt politically or socially is difficult — perhaps impossible — to estimate. But McCarthy's intent was clear. It was to sow suspicion and distrust not merely of these men's political views but of their very character and loyalty.

Conservatives have had potluck with McCarthy too:

(1) He has time and again reflected on the integrity of Dr. James Conant and on Conant's successor at Harvard University, Dr. Nathan Pusey, another middle-of-the-road Republican.

(2) He has challenged the trustworthiness of Senators Taft and Knowland.

(3) He has publicly doubted the veracity of Secretary of State Dulles.

(4) He has questioned the honesty of Assistant Secretary of Defense H. Struve Hensel.

(5) He has subjected Secretary of the Army Stevens to humiliation and ridicule.

By extension, all of these attacks (plus run-ins with Walter Bedell Smith and Harold Stassen) have clearly represented slurs on the competence, integrity, and leadership of President Eisenhower himself.

VI. SOWING THE SEEDS OF DISUNITY ABROAD

Probably no American is more discussed abroad than Senator McCarthy. Sweden's largest and most influential newspaper, the Stockholm *Dagens Nyheter,* reports:

> The unanimous opinion of Europe is that Joseph McCarthy symbolizes exactly the reverse of what America stands for and what we have learned to appreciate. His name is the arch enemy of liberty, and a disgrace to the name of America.

Senator McCarthy has spread disunity in the free world by symbolizing the fanatic forces of unreason which free men abroad fear may be overtaking America. He is not only the American most widely discussed abroad — but also the one most widely feared.

Certainly there is an exaggerated view abroad about the extent of McCarthy's actual political power at home. This view — the result of misinformation, poor reporting, the distortions of distance, combined with a case of Cold War jitters and normally ambivalent feelings about America — is that McCarthy is an American Hitler and is about to take over the country. This view is obviously hysterical. But the fact that it is generally accepted constitutes a serious problem in inter-Allied relations.

But even the more sober voices, such as the Stockholm newspaper we have quoted, view the situation with some measure of alarm. Thus the *Tablet,* the leading Catholic Church journal in England, recently observed:

> Unless the President can silence the Senator, the Republicans will be in difficulties. . . . The world today could not support anything short

of a hard, cold realism guiding the policies of the United States. The time is too serious for Messiahs of either right or left.

A socialist, militantly anti-Communist newspaper in Vienna, the *Arbeiter-Zeitung,* puts it this way:

It is the worst and most ineffectual weapon against Communism — to copy its GPU. No one needs to warn us in Austria . . . what Communist infiltration means and how it should be fought. That is why we protest against McCarthy and his terror. It makes the battle harder for America — and for us.

One of Western Germany's leading conservative newspapers, the *Frankfurter Allgemeine Zeitung,* expresses similar sentiments:

. . . the spread of McCarthyism fills America's friends with increasing anxiety. . . . Forces are growing in America with which we have long been familiar in our less fortunate continent. . . . If these forces should continue to gain ground in America, the leading power of the western world, there would be reason for the gravest anxiety.

The position of all these sober editorialists is summed up by the London *Times,* which asserts that McCarthy has so greatly damaged American interests abroad that he "has become the direct concern of the United States' allies."

It need only be added that McCarthy poses so serious a problem to inter-Allied relations that the National Security Council — responsible to the President for formulating basic American policies — reportedly made a special study of how to cope with this very problem.

The 1953 trip to Europe by Roy Cohn and G. David Schine served only to exacerbate the situation. Their antics, their hectic press conferences, their petulant search for ideological deviationism, their pathetic incompetence in gathering reliable information, caused the chancelleries, parliaments, and editorial offices of all Europe to reverberate with belly-laughs and with angry jeers.

The Stockholm *Dagens Nyheter* wrote:

What the gentlemen possibly might have discovered they have already spoiled by foolishness and arrogance. They have introduced anti-American propaganda far more effective than what possibly could have been accomplished by the Communistic books and persons they were supposed to investigate.

The ultra-conservative *Financial Times* of London called the two young men "scummy snoopers and distempered jackals."

The *Independent Weekly,* an organ of the Church of England, referred to them as "McCarthy's two agents of intolerance and totalitarianism."

In Germany the neutralist *Merkur* of Munich was able to assert that Cohn and Schine had "undermined confidence" in the American government's anti-Communist radio broadcasts beamed behind the Iron Curtain.

This performance alone brought home to Europeans the worst features of the McCarthy impact. It presented America in a ludicrous light and robbed our country of some measure of dignity.

The Communist propaganda machine has adroitly manipulated the specter of McCarthyism to widen even further the gulf between us and our friends. McCarthy has thus played directly into the hands of the Communists. The Munich *Merkur* said:

> It is not known whether Senator McCarthy was helping the Soviets intentionally or not, but the effect of his activities was such that he will probably be made an honorary member of the Communist Party by the Kremlin soon.

Communist propaganda has adapted itself skillfully to the issue of McCarthyism in Europe. This became especially true in March 1954, after McCarthy launched his all-out attack on the United States Army. The cumulative evidence since then clearly indicates that a new propaganda line has been promulgated in the Soviet and satellite press and radio. The line is to exploit rather than oppose McCarthy.

In place of the worn-out lies and clichés about American "Fascism," the Communist propagandists hew more closely to the realities of the situation. With a clever combination of truth and fiction they can now use a flesh-and-blood figure with which to frighten into further submission the miserable subjects whom they tyrannize:

(1) After March 6 Moscow Radio began reporting "the whipping up of hysteria on a nation-wide scale" in the United States.

(2) Warsaw Radio, also in March, compared McCarthy with Hitler. It stressed the purported similarity between Hitler's supporters among the German industrialists and McCarthy's supporters among Texas oil millionaires — "the most reactionary and war-minded section of American monopoly capitalism." The Prague newspaper *Praca* reported to its readers "the reactionary hysteria, the muddy waters of which are flooding the entire public life of the USA."

We in America know that McCarthy is far from taking over this country. We know the limits as well as the extent of his power. We know that the weight of our democratic traditions is more than enough to overwhelm any threat he poses. We know that the chorus of opposition grows daily.

But just as it is infinitely more difficult to refute a lie than to tell it — to wipe off the mud than to sling it — so is it more complicated to convey to our European friends an accurate picture of the real situation, with our profound faith that McCarthy too will pass.

Thus the Senator spreads disunity in the free world, and in doing so he plays directly into the hands of the Communists, whose major aim is to drive a wedge between us and our Allies.

But the Senator is *America's* problem. The reaction of our European friends must necessarily remain secondary for us. It is for us to understand him and the forces he represents — and to cope with them. We do so when we mobilize the essentially conservative values of our democratic society to grapple with the spirit of anti-intellectualism, of vigilantism, of mutual distrust.

For our European friends Senator McCarthy is a bogey-man. Perhaps, under present international circumstances, they would find some other bogey if McCarthy didn't exist. For us in America, however, Senator McCarthy is not and need not be a bogey-man. He is a reality to be confronted and overcome — with the use of reason, of truth, and of sanity.

5. McCarthyism versus Conservatism

Through a continuous process of clarification and refinement, our society has molded a network of institutions — constitutional, legal, political — which embody the restraints of reason and law. Without these restraints, a democratic society is condemned to self-destruction. Unprincipled, unscrupulous political ambition perverts the purposes of a conservative political system because it undermines the *restraints* imposed by that system. In this sense, Senator McCarthy is a radical rather than a conservative, for he poses a threat to the conservative legal and moral values of our society; this, despite the support he has received from many who are conservative in their political and economic viewpoints.

The crux of McCarthy's challenge to conservatism is his use of the lie. The uses of falsehood in an advanced civilization are many and varied. Falsehood even has a certain honored — or at least accepted — position in some of our social and political relations (the white lie, for instance). It is not unknown in the halls of Congress or, for that matter, in the legislative assemblies of the other democracies. But the continuous, brazen, calculated, and unprincipled use of falsehood to destroy all opponents and to advance one's own power becomes a serious threat to the functioning of our political processes. The lie, as used by McCarthy, subverts reason, and consequently upholds unreason; it undermines the law, and leads to lawlessness. When unreason and lawlessness become extreme the conservation of society is in danger.

Senator McCarthy's appeal to unreason and lawlessness constitutes a threat to the stability of governmental institutions, to the prerogatives of government, and to the rights of the citizen as guaranteed by the Constitution. Above all, in its loose use of the charge of treason, it is a call to civil disunion and thus a threat to the peace of democratic society.

A survey of McCarthy's activities in the brief period of his committee chairmanship leaves one with a feeling of wonder and amazement at the extent of his successful assaults on the stability of government institutions. We have seen the effects of the damage he has inflicted, in terms of morale, security procedures, manpower recruitment, and the day-to-day operation of the State Department, the Foreign Service, the Army, and the information program. The Senator's investigation of Fort Monmouth is perhaps the most concentrated and striking illustration of his use of deceit, innuendo, and falsehood. But the Army-McCarthy hearings, in which the Senator himself was a party to the dispute, reflected the extent to which the entire Army establishment, from the Secretary on down, was diverted from its urgent duties and forced to defend itself against his assaults.

The hazards of government service have become, both for those who are in it and for those who might consider it, problematic. Government agencies are finding it difficult to recruit distinguished men of affairs for service in the public interest. What can be the effect, on such men, of Senator McCarthy's hounding of Secretary of the Army Stevens, a leading industrialist, and Assistant Defense Secretary Hensel, a prominent attorney and businessman? An answer has been supplied by Dr. Charles Mayo, chief of the Mayo Clinic and an Eisenhower-appointed member of the United States delegation to the United Nations. In reaction to the Army-McCarthy imbroglio he said: "It's getting to be a most difficult thing in this country to accept appointment to Government service. You subject yourself to such indignities and insults and untruths." Stable, respected men may think twice and three times — and even then turn down an invitation to serve the government.[1]

But the problem of the stability of government institutions is not exhausted by the hazards encountered by leading appointive officials like Stevens, Hensel, and Mayo. It is most graphically illustrated by the situation of the nameless men for whom public service is not a short-term affair but a career. The stability of the Foreign Service is gravely affected when there is a drop of 50 per cent in applications for the Service — as was the case in 1953. Scientists seek to leave Army employment because of McCarthy's harassment of their colleagues at Fort Monmouth. The stability of the whole Civil Service is jeopardized precisely because of the uncertainty and insecurity engendered by the Senator's irresponsible assaults. Throughout the government, some loyal, competent civil servants — Army officers, propaganda experts, technicians, public-administration officials — are trying to get out as soon as they can,

---

[1] Even before the McCarthy era, the government was embarrassed by recruiting difficulties. For instance, thirty-two men turned down the office of Assistant Secretary of State before the thirty-third candidate could be persuaded to accept the important post on February 1, 1950 (eight days before McCarthy's Wheeling speech). In other words, Senator McCarthy made a normally difficult situation considerably more difficult.

and fewer candidates than ever are trying to get in. A government that cannot hold and attract able officials is a government whose effective operation and stability are endangered.

The threat that Senator McCarthy poses to our constitutional norms and guarantees is even more insidious than his disruption of government stability. For it is in precisely this area that he descends into flagrant lawlessness. This lawlessness takes two forms: encroachment upon the Executive Branch and usurpation of judicial powers; and abandonment or rejection of the usages of constitutional liberty.

McCarthy's "deal" with the Greek shipowners stands out as a blatant example of encroachment on Executive Branch prerogatives in the field of foreign affairs. But other equally telling examples have been mentioned in the preceding chapters:

(1) During the early stages of his investigation of the International Information Administration, McCarthy called Under-Secretary of State Walter Bedell Smith on the carpet for issuing an administrative memorandum that confirmed certain discretionary rights to employees in dealing with Congressional committees. The Senator was much displeased and took the memorandum as a direct affront. It was repudiated the next day.

(2) Along similar lines was the Senator's bullying of Bradley Connors, the policy chief of the International Information Administration, culminating in a virtual order to Connors to issue a directive on the handling of Communist and controversial material in overseas libraries. Connors complied the same day.

(3) The appointment of Scott McLeod, an avowed "McCarthy man," as the State Department's Personnel and Security Officer was on all sides taken as a concession by the administration to McCarthy's views and standards on security matters. What this signified with regard to the practice of all the lesser McLeods throughout the government became clear in the Army's hasty, ill-considered response to McCarthy's pressures at Fort Monmouth. As we have noted, the Senator's entry into the picture resulted in an upsurge of careless suspensions.

(4) Another amazing example of McCarthy's encroachment on the Executive Branch was this: By November 1953 McCarthy had strengthened his position vis-à-vis the administration to such an extent that the Secretary of the Army, by his own admission, sought to gauge the Senator's reaction to his contemplated demotion of a general. We may never know whether it was the Senator's expressed displeasure that ultimately dissuaded the Sec-

retary from making the move. But the fact that the Secretary should even have taken into consideration the Senator's reaction is itself indicative of the extent to which McCarthy's power had reached into the Executive Branch.

(5) And the most insidious illustration of encroachment on the Executive Branch is the extensive penetration of government agencies by McCarthy's "American underground." It first came to light in the Voice of America hearings and was dramatically confirmed during the special Senate investigation of the Army-McCarthy clash. The very existence of such a network is in itself, as President Eisenhower remarked at the time, a grave threat to the processes of orderly government and democratic concepts of loyalty. It is an equally grave threat to the morale of loyal civil servants. But its worst feature is the brazen, mock-heroic manner in which Senator McCarthy conducts and exploits the operation of this "underground." When confronted with the revelation that a confidential summary of a top-secret FBI document had been found in his possession, not only did he admit the fact, but he boasted of it — and he warned that no power on earth could force him to divulge the source of his information. Few greater threats to the structure of constitutional government can be imagined than this wanton disregard of the separation of powers.

Senator McCarthy has transformed the investigating subcommittee into an arbitrary, *ad hoc* court of law. Cases are not so much investigated as tried — in a loose, informal way. It is the technique of the kangaroo court. Contrast any public hearing conducted by Senator McCarthy with the hearing conducted by Senator Richard Russell into the dismissal of General MacArthur. One can only speculate on the sensational charges of sabotage, espionage, and subversion with which McCarthy would have accompanied that investigation, had he been the chairman. His investigations are characterized by badgering of witnesses, arbitrary and distorted summaries of testimony, loaded questions, unfair innuendoes, and the admission of derogatory testimony and evidence without opportunity for rebuttal. All of these are contrary to the spirit of a Constitution and a society predicated on fair play and due process of law.

In committee, on the Senate floor, on the public platform, Senator McCarthy's recourse to unfounded and unsubstantiated accusations and insinuations outrages the basic principles of a conservative system of law and politics. It is an even greater outrage because this practice rarely allows the victimized citizen any redress in a court of law or in the public press. Assistant Secretary of Defense Hensel, for example, has in an affidavit strongly repudiated Senator McCarthy's attacks on his integrity. But the Senator need never deprive himself of his immunity and come forward to face a libel suit in a court of law. Such behavior is a direct challenge to the power of the law to protect the rights and liberties of citizens.

But it is Senator McCarthy's unsubstantiated charges of treason that provide the most startling illustration of his use of falsehood in the assault on the two-party system. His famous 1954 series of Lincoln Day speeches on "Twenty Years of Treason" were the culmination of a long line of such accusations and insinuations leveled by McCarthy against Democratic administrations and leaders. The Senator has here used his characteristic technique: to add to the kernel of truth — namely, the mistakes and grave errors of judgment for which Presidents Roosevelt and Truman were responsible — a host of exaggerations, distortions, and outright lies. The charges of treason were so outrageous that President Eisenhower made no bones about dissociating himself from them.

The unfounded charge of treason is a call to civil disunion calculated to destroy the opposition. If heeded, its ultimate effect would be the destruction of the legal and moral values whose existence and operation depend entirely on public consensus. The last time the citizens of this country waved "the bloody flag" was during the Reconstruction period — and the nation has not yet recovered from the effects. During the present period of protracted world crisis, with American leadership indispensable to the security and survival of the free world, this nation can surely ill afford another such ordeal.

As Walter Lippmann has cogently remarked, treason is a mortal crime — and a false accusation of treason must surely be a mortal sin, against the accused individual and against society. No other charge is so likely to stir up public passions, and its ultimate effect is to create a wall of suspicion and hatred between one-half of the nation and the other. The use of the calculated falsehood in this respect represents the ultimate appeal to unreason.

The false charge of treason has been introduced by Senator McCarthy at a time of national frustration, of bitterness over the casualties of war. In an earlier time of anger, bitterness, and passion, a wiser leader had the courage, the magnanimity and the vision to call upon the nation to bind up its wounds — "to do all which may achieve and cherish a just and lasting peace among ourselves."

6. Is Senator McCarthy a Totalitarian?

What manner of political man is Senator McCarthy? In that question are rooted the hopes and fears of millions of people in this country. Senator McCarthy has deeply stirred the passions of this nation, more than any other politician since the Franklin Roosevelt of the New Deal era. It is a token of the Senator's political virility and substance that he has had the power to stir his opponents to such bitterness, his partisans to such adulation.

Senator McCarthy is endowed with many talents, including a remarkably retentive memory (especially for small details), a native shrewdness, and a sure instinct that enables him to probe and exploit an opponent's weakness. He is a brilliant tactician, a highly skilled maneuverer and in-fighter, an astonishingly able parliamentarian on the Senate floor and in committee, and — despite his lack of polish and finesse — an effective figure on the public platform. He is clearly single-minded of purpose and to many people a man of considerable personal charm. All of these qualities make him a formidable figure.

Who are his admirers and his enemies? And what do they make of him? What do they take his purpose to be, and how does it fit in with their own purposes?

Practically everyone has an opinion about Senator McCarthy, and if we were to move through the spectrum of American politics we would find the gamut of strong feelings and opinions about him. At one extreme are the lunatic-fringe, native fascist groups, at the other extreme the Communists. Neither of these groups lies within the range of authentic American politics, and their respective support of and opposition to Senator McCarthy is not as easily explicable as might appear.

What the Senator's enemies and partisans make of him is an interesting and important question, the answer to which can shed considerable light on the composition of present-day political forces in the United States. But a proper analysis of the Senator's support and opposition must be a function of a more fundamental question: What does McCarthy make of himself? What is he, and what is he after?

Senator McCarthy is not a unique phenomenon in American political history. He stems from the frontier tradition rooted in the Midwest. The frontiersmen, rejecting the life-patterns of the East, carved out their own fortunes and produced a new image of individualism in America. The hero of this image was independent, self-reliant, virile, strong, simple, and direct. This rough-and-ready customer had little time for education, considered culture suspiciously effeminate, and was ignorant or contemptuous of Old World refinement and Eastern gentility. The politics that emerged in the Midwest, populist and conservative alike, was closely related to this image of individualism. It never laid claim to a broad international — or even national — perspective. Its base was always that of local need and interest; it was deeply suspicious of incursions by outsiders and strangers; and its outlook on larger problems was determined largely by the simple, direct relations that the people of the region had to each other and to their land. In this atmosphere, simple, unsophisticated, and uncomplicated panaceas could be put forward as solutions for large, complex problems. The region understandably became a breeding ground for demagogues and demagoguery.

Senator McCarthy is an ambitious politician of this school. With this tradition as a base, he proceeded to discard some of the accepted conventions of political restraint, to enlarge upon similarly accepted traditions of political license — until he finally unleashed his ambitions in all their force. This kind of drive requires the calculated use of any means for its self-realization. Power and status are its ends. And the clever exploitation of a popular issue and mood make of such an ambitious politician a demagogue.

Senator McCarthy as a power-seeking demagogue is clearly a force to be contended with. But does that make the Senator himself a totalitarian? When the *Daily Worker* calls McCarthy "the American Hitler," it is merely using the same sort of stereotyped slander amalgam (see Chapter 3) to which the Senator himself is addicted. In the past the Communist press in this and other countries has discovered many "American Hitlers," among them Franklin D. Roosevelt and Harry Truman. In the future it will find others. Communism, in its efforts to confuse the friends of freedom, is always in search of "fascist" scarecrows on which to drape the soiled and faded rags of its fear-propaganda.

The attribution of totalitarian proclivities to the Senator proceeds from two other, more serious groups — one friendly, the other un-friendly. In the first place, McCarthy's successes in charging the American political atmosphere with divisive tensions and in causing damage to some government institutions have led many fearful liberals to conclude that he is indeed a totalitarian. Such liberals — and they are in no sense pro-Communists or fellow-travelers — took a long time to recognize the evil threat of the Communist conspiracy; even today they still fail to face up to the need for a vigorous internal-security program. Norman Thomas has incisively characterized them as the liberals "who may be re-luctantly persuaded that Alger Hiss is guilty, but never can forgive Whittaker Chambers."

Some of these persons have relinquished their powers of discrim-ination to a point where they equate Communism and McCarthy-ism, as to the evils they represent and the threats they pose. Such liberals — and they are unhappily numerous — missed the boat twice: in recognizing the nature of the international Communist conspiracy too late and inadequately, and in exaggerating the power of Senator McCarthy. In their failure to understand what makes him operate the way he does, they lessen the chance of oppos-ing him effectively. When they label McCarthy totalitarian, they lend credence to the "demon-theory" of history with which they reproach McCarthy's followers. And in making all these mis-takes these people confuse and obscure the real issues. They lend aid and comfort to the Communists, who delight in stirring up hysteria, political cynicism, and impotence. And they make it easier for the Senator to persist in his spray-gun tactics of attacking all liberals — as well as all his opponents — as Communists or pro-Communists.

In the second place, some of McCarthy's neophyte intellectual spokesmen and sophisticated apologists hanker to make a totali-tarian of him. This tendency has been expressed most clearly in the best-selling book *McCarthy and His Enemies,* by William F. Buckley, Jr., and L. Brent Bozell, a remarkably able defense of the Senator's record.[1] In a chapter entitled "The New Conformity," in which they argue for a new American orthodoxy, the authors analyze the significance of one of McCarthy's most famous cam-paign speeches. As we noted earlier, the Senator in October 1952 delivered a televised attack on Adlai Stevenson and a half-dozen of his liberal advisers, among them Arthur Schlesinger, Jr., James

[1] Chicago: Henry Regnery Company, 1954. See Appendix A (page 148 below) for an analysis of the book's thesis.

Wechsler, and Bernard DeVoto. Buckley and Bozell contend that McCarthy's "objection to these men was not that they were Communists, or even pro-Communists, but that they were *Liberals* . . . and that this was sufficient reason for rejecting" the Democratic candidate (italics added). The authors grant that only McCarthy could say "whether the speech was a conscious effort to narrow the limits of tolerable opinion so as to exclude left-wing Liberals." They tend to believe this was not his intent — that he was only making a typical campaign speech. "But," they add, "it may well be that we have not heard the last of this idea. Some day, the patience of America may at last be exhausted, and we will strike out against Liberals."

This view, coupled with the authors' conviction that "the man who frustrates American policy *without* wicked intent is no less objectionable than the man who frustrates it *with* wicked intent" (italics in the original), certainly smacks of an absolutist political dogma that has elements of a totalitarianism. But these sophisticated apologists for Senator McCarthy may be indulging in wishful thinking when they hope to impute these intentions to him.

Buckley and Bozell of course make a mistake when they maintain that McCarthy is after the "Liberals" primarily. He is out to get not only liberals but conservatives as well, as shown by his persistent attacks on President Eisenhower and his associates. The Senator, encouraged by his successes, seeks to impugn the motives of anyone who stands in his way, or who might do so. Thus his recent aspersions on the integrity of Assistant Secretary of Defense H. Struve Hensel, a conservative entrepreneur, are no different from his aspersions on the loyalty of his liberal opponents — which are merely an extension of McCarthy's instinctively sure exploitation of the popular anti-Communist mood.

The "wishful thinkers" of the right and the left do not, of course, exhaust the categories of Senator McCarthy's friends and enemies. Among his most vigorous opponents are those that might be called "hard" liberals, who believe that ruthless, uncontrolled ambition itself threatens the fabric of a democratic society. One could mention such old-line labor leaders as George Meany, Walter Reuther, James Carey, David Dubinsky, or such leaders of the Liberal Party as George Counts and Adolf Berle. All of them have had long, consistent, and successful careers of exposing and destroying Communist influence; they do not view the current situation hysterically; they have never been guilty of subscribing to the serious errors of some of their liberal associates; and they do not mistake demagogic ambition for totalitarianism.

If people who have been careless about applying the word "fascist" to McCarthy will recall the salient facts of Huey Long's life and works, the critical differences between a power-seeking demagogue and an authentic American fascist will become immediately apparent.

Huey Long was not just a demagogue (although he was that too). He was an ideologue, a theoretician, a planner, an organizer. His library was well stocked with the theoretical literature of both Marxism and Fascism. On the football field of Louisiana State University at Baton Rouge, Huey's cadets marched to the strains of Mussolini's Fascist hymn, "La Giovanezza." Huey Long had a program — "Share the Wealth" — aimed at building a mass base of poor farmers and mill workers. He organized and led a movement which had recruited a substantial following in a half-dozen Southern states before he died.

Neither Wisconsin nor Washington has seen anything like that during McCarthy's twenty years in public life.

However, the argument that Senator McCarthy is a totalitarian, or a potential one, can muster some impressive evidence, and it bears closer examination.

Definition of totalitarianism

If the authentic anti-Communist is obliged to draw lines of distinction between Communism, socialism, and liberalism, it is equally incumbent on him to draw similar lines of distinction between totalitarianism and other forms of authoritarianism.

Totalitarianism is not equivalent to dictatorship, one-party rule, or a military regime. Organized societies, in the several millennia of their existence, have known all three of those forms of government and others similar to them, and have subjected them to much analysis. But it is significant that neither the Hellenes — the classical creators of political philosophy — nor their successors of the Renaissance and the modern period, beginning with Machiavelli, mentioned the concept of totalitarianism. They did not know it.

David Rousset[2] has written: "Normal men do not know that

[2] Rousset is the distinguished French author of two of the most penetrating analyses (based on personal experience) of concentration-camp existence under the Nazis: *Les Jours de Notre Mort* and *The Other Kingdom,* both published in 1947. In recent years he organized and headed an International Commission to Investigate Slave Labor, which in 1952 conducted a world-famous trial, in Brussels, decisively exposing, documenting, and condemning Soviet slave-labor camps.

everything is possible." By that he meant that the ultimate in human depravity is not only conceivable but possible. Totalitarianism is a unique product of the twentieth century which demonstrates that everything is indeed possible, which plumbs the depths of human depravity. It is the culmination of a number of modern historical forces, not the least of which is the process of atomization of society which in our time has made it possible to translate individual men into the heretofore unknown phenomenon of mass-man. Nazism, Fascism, Communism are examples of totalitarian movements.

Totalitarianism is not simply a political phenomenon. It is a spiritual movement, possessing comprehensive ideological scope and global political aspirations. It demands of its adherents unquestioning, inflexible discipline and an all-embracing loyalty; organization is the *sine qua non* of the totalitarian movement. To this end it establishes a powerful machinery of propaganda and operates within an atmosphere of created violence. When the movement attains power, propaganda and violence are transformed into the nearly total thought-control and terror with which the total state wages perpetual war on its own subjects.

Totalitarianism depends both on the ability of the leader to harness political power and on the political susceptibility of the followers. No one can judge precisely whether any man is a potential totalitarian leader unless it is known that the society within which he moves has political characteristics that would make it prone to submit to totalitarianism.

Is Senator McCarthy an actual or potential totalitarian leader and does he lead a totalitarian movement?

1. Methods

It has been pointed out that McCarthy employs some of the techniques characteristically used by totalitarian leaders. However, viewed historically, many of these methods were not the creation of the totalitarians. Often they have been part of the arsenal of traditional demagogic tactics — even in the United States. Indeed politics in this country has been a traditionally violent pastime, on the verbal level at least. Thomas Paine once described George Washington as "treacherous in private friendship and a hypocrite in public life." And a political opponent once called Thomas Jefferson "an atheist, an adulterer, and a robber."

What Senator McCarthy has done is to extend to an extreme degree the limits of accepted traditions of political license. But the use of demagogic techniques is, by itself, no certain indication of totalitarian intent.

2. The "Movement" Around McCarthy

The Senator's following includes an unlikely combination of diverse — and often inherently conflicting — elements of support. Certain striking parallels with Hitler's following have convinced some observers of McCarthy's potentialities as a totalitarian.

Who are his supporters and what is the quality of their support?

(a) There is, first, a negligible fringe, native-fascist element led by Gerald L. K. Smith and others of his ilk — "apostles of discord," as they have been called. The very existence of their vociferous support, never repudiated by McCarthy with vigor or persistence, may indicate something about his motivations — although to build a case on it would be the worst kind of guilt-by-association technique. And it is at least equally significant that the Senator has not had any direct dealings with these unsavory people.

(b) McCarthy has come to be regarded as a spokesman for the historico-ethnic resentments and aspirations of large segments of the German-American and Irish Catholic population, as well as of midwestern isolationists in general. Some of his strongest support comes from these groups, and his appeal for them is a natural one.

No doubt McCarthy addresses himself to what is called a "nationalist" audience. But he cannot be said to represent that audience in nearly as direct and unequivocal a manner as — for example — Senator Everett M. Dirksen. In fact McCarthy's voting record on foreign policy is by no means as consistently "isolationist" as that of Senators Dirksen or Bricker.[3]

Indeed one might say that Senator McCarthy's record in this field represents a significant shift in the nature of latter-day isolationism. This is no longer the unqualified body of thought it used to be in the days of Borah, Wheeler, and the early Vandenberg. Inevitably the world position of the United States and its irrevocable international commitments have injected a note of internationalism into all but the most perfervid isolationist views. McCarthy's record reflects that change.

And so it is fair to say, we believe, that current isolationism is less likely to be diverted into a rabid, extreme political form than it was in the past.

[3] See Appendix A.

(c) For a number of years the Senator has been receiving the political and financial support of a number of very successful Texas oil and cattle men. Some of these men have also had connections with the Gerald L. K. Smith crowd. Most of them have not. This backing from traditionally independent, individualistic Texans is indeed anomalous because McCarthy is an outsider, a Northerner, a Republican — and a Catholic to boot.

But this support is beginning to wane. A survey in the April 1954 issue of *Fortune* magazine reported that, although the Senator's popularity was still strong in the Lone Star State, several of his previously ardent influential supporters there were beginning to back away from him, especially after he renewed his attack on the Army. And the Army-McCarthy hearings harmed him further in this area.

The same survey also reported growing disaffection for the Senator among conservative business circles in the Southeast, and indeed in most parts of the country. Among these influential business and industrial leaders, McCarthy's high point was probably reached during the Presidential campaign of 1952. In their eyes he has been on the downgrade ever since.

The *Fortune* report emphasized another very significant point. Senator McCarthy's appeal for business leaders has consisted almost exclusively in his self-portrait as the tough, effective anti-Communist. But if he were to develop a broader demagogic appeal on domestic issues, appealing to the people with promises of material welfare — in other words, if he were to build a domestic program as Hitler did along totalitarian lines — the pro-McCarthy business-men state emphatically that they would then waste no time in cutting their ties with him.

(d) There are a number of Republican Party leaders who privately loathe the Senator — and would not in the last analysis accept his leadership — who lend him tacit or overt support either out of fear or out of calculation. (They are tolerably happy with him when he restricts his attacks to the Democrats.)

However, since McCarthy's assault on the Eisenhower administration has become unmistakably clear, and especially since the administration has begun to move against him, these elements are beginning to cool toward McCarthy — cautiously but noticeably.

(e) Public-opinion polls have indicated that less-educated and lower-income groups have tended more than others to support the Senator. This has been interpreted by some observers as a possible parallel to the ominous backing given Hitler by the German. *Lumpenproletariat.*[4]

But in this area, too, the Senator's support is beginning to wane. For example, the Gallup polls for January 15 and March 15, 1954, indicate an interesting shift away from McCarthy among manual workers. In January, 50 per cent indicated approval of the Senator, 23 per cent disapproval, and 27 per cent no opinion. In March, 45 per cent indicated approval, 34 per cent disapproval, while the percentage of those without opinions had dropped to 21.

This shift is paralleled by a similar change among all other socio-economic groups interviewed by the Gallup researchers — except for the farmers. (Among them McCarthy's approval percentage rose during the two months from 48 to 53, his disapproval percentage dropped from 29 to 26, and the "no opinion" percentage dropped from 23 to 21. This divergence from the general pattern can be explained by the fact that McCarthy's greatest strength still lies in the farming communities of the Midwest. The *Fortune* survey corroborated this fact, although it also noted that the trend in the business community of the Midwest had begun to conform to the national pattern of a drift away from McCarthy.)

By all indications the Senator began to travel downward in the opinion of most groups even more swiftly during the Army-McCarthy hearings.

Here, then, is another instance of lack of support for a drive toward totalitarian power.

(f) There has undoubtedly been a large segment of middle-of-the-road conservative opinion which the Senator's pyrotechnics have dazzled into believing that he is a dedicated and effective anti-Communist.

But as the facts of McCarthy's basic indifference to Communism are revealed, this element is being driven even farther from him. This drift is reflected in the *Fortune* survey, the Gallup polls, and the editorial pages of the conservative press throughout the United States.

---

[4] This consisted of the uprooted and desperate elements of the petty *bourgeoisie* and white-collar class and the unemployed lower strata of the working class that Hitler transformed into an energized, organized mass movement. Incidentally, Hitler's success in creating this mass base for his totalitarian organization was a realistic contradiction of Karl Marx's prediction that the *Lumpenproletariat* can play no role in a revolutionary movement.

(g) A distinct but more ambiguous category requires special mention here. It includes a number of distinguished, now-conservative, ex-Communist intellectuals, like Eugene Lyons and Max Eastman, as well as a number of conservative intellectuals who were never Communists. These men are themselves responsible anti-totalitarians who do not impute totalitarian motives to McCarthy. They are not so much *pro*-McCarthyites as anti-anti-McCarthyites (opponents of all who oppose McCarthy).

These are men who are surely not taken in by McCarthy's lies. They have no taste for his methods. Nevertheless they tend to be sympathetic to McCarthy — and precisely because of their early disillusionment with Communism. For these were men whose anti-Communist voices cried in the desert of naively idealistic liberalism of the 1930's and 1940's. In the felicitous phrase of John Chamberlain, they were considered "premature anti-Communists."

When many liberals found it fashionable to create Popular Fronts and United Fronts with the Communists in the 1930's, these men cried out, unheard, against the GPU's murderous assaults on the non-Bolshevik elements of Republican Spain.

When many found it fashionable to extol the Stalin Constitution, these men sought, unavailingly, to point up the lessons of the Soviet purge trials.

When many liberals praised the war-time alliance with "our great democratic Soviet ally," these men grimly but unsuccessfully tried to call attention to the scores of slave-labor camps all over the Soviet territory.

When many liberals dreamed of a Soviet "desire for peace," these men carefully demonstrated the immutable, aggressive, imperialist aims of Soviet policy ever since the days of the Bolshevik Revolution.

When their warnings went unheeded, these men naturally felt a bitter revulsion against the "know-nothing" brand of liberalism. This feeling was assuaged, to a certain extent, when Senator McCarthy began his campaign to persuade large segments of the American people that he was conducting a singlehanded "fight for America." The anti-anti-McCarthyites quite correctly saw that many of the protests against McCarthy's "methods" were really protests against any investigation of Communists. It was the spurious and reprehensible nature of such protests — coming from the same quarters that had always failed to heed their warnings — that inclined the anti-anti-McCarthyites mistakenly to equate "Mc-

Carthyism" with the vigorous investigation and exposure of Communists.[5]

The genuinely conservative persons who oppose all opponents of McCarthy do their own cause the same kind of injustice as do the genuinely liberal persons who oppose all opponents of Communism. Just as the latter mistakenly assume that a defense of civil liberties requires an unthinking defense of the beliefs of Communists under attack, so the former mistakenly assume that the espousal of effective investigation of Communists requires an undiscriminating defense of McCarthy. Such undifferentiated beliefs cripple otherwise legitimate positions.

3. Organization

Senator McCarthy has never shown himself willing or able to organize a movement of any kind. (As we have seen, even if he had tried he would have found that the elements of totalitarian support were lacking.) He has certainly not organized — or made any attempt in the direction of organizing — a revolutionary élite or a "storm troop."

Nor does McCarthy have a propaganda mechanism ready to hand. It is true that he has a journalistic claque — but important elements of this group are beginning to fail him. Of those that remain loyal, exceedingly few could by any stretch of the imagination be considered supporters of totalitarianism.

Furthermore the United States is not passing through a reign of terror or hysteria, Professor Henry Steele Commager to the contrary notwithstanding. (Publication of his book *Freedom, Loyalty, Dissent* — and of this present volume — is itself convincing testimony to this.) However, it must be noted that *Fortune*'s survey did provide some evidence of McCarthy's power to engender fear. Of 253 business executives approached by the *Fortune* reporter, only 88 were willing to speak for the record; many were willing to talk only on a not-for-attribution basis; and some declined altogether to discuss the Senator.

In fact, this sorry attitude reflects less on the Senator's strength

[5] The mistake of this equation is startlingly evident in the contrast between the work of the Senate Permanent Subcommittee on Investigations (McCarthy) and the Senate Internal Security Subcommittee (McCarran and Jenner). Contrast, for example, the completely irrelevant job performed by McCarthy on the Voice of America with the detailed, factual exposé of the Institute of Pacific Relations by McCarran and his subcommittee's chief counsel, Robert Morris.

than on the unnecessarily cautious and timid approach of the executives interviewed by *Fortune*. There is, of course, no real ground
for this kind of apprehension. And it can be expected to give way
as the Senator continues to lose ground among the population
generally.

Not only has Senator McCarthy shown no inclination to build
a movement, but he has displayed a positive genius for alienating
supporters. Charles R. Seaborne, an industrialist in McCarthy's
home-town district of Appleton, Wisconsin, and an old friend and
supporter of the Senator, was taken aback in July 1953 by Mc-
Carthy's attack on an equally respected Appleton favorite, Dr.
Nathan Pusey, newly appointed president of Harvard University.
Seaborne sent the Senator a telegram:

> RE YOUR RELEASE ON PUSEY. FEEL [IT] MOST UNIN-
> FORMED AND UNADVISED. SORRY THAT YOU ARE LETTING
> DOWN SO MANY OLD FRIENDS. HOPE YOU CAN EXPLAIN.

McCarthy's immediate response, received by Seaborne the following day, said:

> AM CURIOUS TO KNOW WHAT OLD FRIENDS ARE BEING
> LET DOWN BY THE EXPOSURE OF BIGOTED, INTOLERANT,
> MUD-SLINGING ENEMY OF MINE.

This is not the behavior of a movement-builder.

4. Ideology

Joe McCarthy has been a public figure for over twenty years in
Wisconsin and Washington. During this entire period he has never
authored a serious analysis of any political problem or put forth
any solid, programmatic statement.

In fact McCarthy has no program. A single plank does not
build a platform. And, as we have seen, even anti-Communism is
for him less a plank than an instrument with which to exploit a
fearful mood.

True, the Communists could become for McCarthy a "key to
history." The Jews played this role for Nazism, just as Trotsky
and other "deviationists" did for Stalinism. But McCarthy's anti-
Communism could not become a "key to history" without a
philosophy of history.

This is another way of saying that McCarthy lacks not only a program for state action but an ideology as well.

His inability to organize a movement and his total lack of program and ideology are closely related to his inability, or evident unwillingness, to complete a job — and his exclusive job has purportedly been the conduct of the anti-Communist crusade.

Who ever heard of a successful totalitarian without persistence in his main task?

5. Anti-Semitism

If Senator McCarthy were to become a totalitarian, his whole record indicates that he would be a totalitarian of the "right" rather than of the "left." As the example of Hitler demonstrates, anti-Semitism is often an integral part of that brand of totalitarianism; and persecution of minority groups has been a consistent totalitarian characteristic.

And yet McCarthy has gone to considerable pains to try to demonstrate that he is not an anti-Semite. He has, for example, surrounded himself with Jewish aides and advisers. We need mention only his aides Roy Cohn and G. David Schine, the columnists George Sokolsky and Walter Winchell, and the first-rank Hearst executive Richard Berlin.

It is of course conceivable that McCarthy's demonstrative "philo-Semitism" is merely a pose, a cynical maneuver designed to mislead citizens in whose eyes a leader's manifestation of religious bigotry would instantly discredit him. But, if so, McCarthy has deprived himself of a valuable asset that would make him particularly attractive to the very elements who would be most likely to support a totalitarian movement under his leadership.

Senator McCarthy publicly eschewed anti-Semitism at the very height of his career, during the period when anti-Semitism in combination with all the other conceivably favorable factors might have been exploited in organizing a movement. This fact testifies not only to the disrepute of anti-Semitism today but to the absence of this particular virus in the Senator's political make-up.

6. The Intellectual Elite

A characteristic and significant element of totalitarian movements has always been the influential group of uprooted intellectuals they have attracted and placed in positions of power and leadership.

McCarthy can lay claim to the allegiance of no such group. Certainly Pegler, Sokolsky, and Winchell are neither intellectual nor elite. On the other hand, such genuine intellectuals as those associated with the *Freeman* magazine are neither uprooted (all of them apparently being well adjusted to the socio-economic structure of America) nor pro-McCarthy (many of them being really anti-anti-McCarthy, which is, as we have seen, an altogether different matter.) After the beginning of 1953, the *Freeman* itself did not attempt to defend Senator McCarthy, but confined itself to exposing what it asserted to be exaggerations and misstatements by his opponents.

An equally significant indication of the Senator's failure to attract an intellectual following is the position of the Catholic intellectuals in the United States. By and large, they are overwhelmingly anti-McCarthy. This is true of the *Commonweal,* the liberal weekly edited by Catholic laymen, and equally of such conservative journals as Notre Dame University's scholarly quarterly, *Review of Politics,* and the Jesuit weekly, *America.*

7. *The Political Context*

Senator McCarthy — as shrewd an operator as the political arena provides today — must be aware that the weight of the American political tradition and current political respectability preclude a successful totalitarianism, or even a successful authoritarianism.

The American constitutional system and public opinion together constitute a subtly self-correcting mechanism that has always succeeded in checking itself in time to avoid the plunge into the abyss of political extremism. There have been demagogues before in the United States. But each time a Huey Long, a Father Coughlin, a Gerald L. K. Smith has appeared, he has been confronted and overcome, and the structure and spirit of constitutionalism have been reinforced through the ordeal.

In this sense American constitutionalism is comparable to British constitutionalism. The provisions of the United States Constitution only provide the foundation for a tradition. It is the spirit in which the basic document is interpreted — applied in the laws and in social and political institutions — and the manner in which threats to the Constitution are met that create our tradition of constitutionalism. That tradition becomes stronger with the passage of time and with the confrontation of specific challenges.

This is the elementary lesson that any ambitious politician must learn: he must operate within the norms of political respectability as defined by the constitutional tradition. If he fails to do so, he must sooner or later pay the penalty of public resentment.

Thus Senator McCarthy, in order to maintain his power and status, must continue to operate within the confines of the Republican Party. He would destroy himself politically if he put himself at the head of a splinter lunatic-fringe grouping clearly outside the limits of political respectability.

Shrewd as he is, McCarthy could conceivably destroy himself in some such way. Rational calculation is of course not the only element in politics; if it were, politics would be not an art or a tricky game of chance but a science. And McCarthy has often shown signs of a peculiar tendency to strike out wildly, unreasonably, and unnecessarily at real or imagined obstacles. Witness, for example, his gross insult to General Zwicker, or his predictably unsuccessful diversionary attack on H. Struve Hensel, or his unexpected charges against a young Republican attorney, Frederick Fisher. These gratuitous attacks have cost him no little in public sympathy and have made him unnecessary enemies. Such behavior is essentially visceral rather than rational. And thus it is not inconceivable that Senator McCarthy should unthinkingly destroy himself by a succession of such maneuvers.

However, if we can assume that rational calculation rather than visceral reaction will, on the whole, continue to guide the Senator in the future as in the past, then it is safe to say that McCarthy will restrict himself to the orbit of Republican politics. To do otherwise would clearly result in his self-destruction.

This very necessity defines the limits of McCarthy's ambition. He may indeed aspire to leadership of the Republican Party. The White House may be his goal—there being nowhere else for this ambitious politician to go except down. At that point, if McCarthy is to retain and expand his following, it will be increasingly necessary for him to make policy commitments on both foreign and domestic issues. From the safe ground of anti-Communism, which has hitherto furnished the lowest common denominator of his support, he will have to move out into the more vulnerable area occupied by any politician who answers Cold War questions in terms of what, when, how, and where. In short, McCarthy will have to clothe the naked nihilism of a power politician with at least the shadow of a program.

But any such move in that direction would betoken a fatal split and rupture of the Republican Party, with McCarthy in control of only a small rump. Short of effectuating such a split, the Senator probably aspires, through the control of his small bloc within the Party, to exercise a balance-of-power role in Party councils.

But even this role, because of its inherent ambiguity, contains certain dangers both to McCarthy and to the Republican Party. For if, as would be most likely, he were to throw his weight toward the "conservative" rather than the "liberal" wing of the Party, he would almost inevitably doom the Party to electoral defeat and consequently achieve his own ultimate repudiation as a factor of importance in the Party.

For one thing is clear about the Republican Party: "me-tooism" is not a dirty word except in Colonel Robert R. McCormick's political lexicon. It reflects the serious recognition by the Republican Party of the genuine temper of the American people. That is why since 1940 it has been the liberal East-and-West-Coast element of the Party that has consistently captured Presidential nominations and ultimately electoral victory. (Willkie in 1940, Dewey in 1944, Dewey and Warren in 1948, Eisenhower and Nixon in 1952.)

Actually, the conservative wing of the Republican Party appeared to have lost its last hope of victory in 1936, with Roosevelt's thunderous defeat of Alfred M. Landon. Since then, not even as distinguished, intelligent, and forceful a figure as Robert A. Taft was able to win his party's nomination. In the light of the Eisenhower victory at the 1952 Republican convention and the electoral victory that fall, it seems safe to predict that the Republicans must remain committed to the candidates of the liberal wing if they hope to repeat their electoral success.

Thus, if McCarthy could succeed in upsetting the internal balance of the party to such an extent as to result in the nomination of a "conservative-wing" candidate, the party would be likely to lose at the polls — and this would almost inevitably lead to the repudiation of even a balance-of-power role for McCarthy. Whoever would occupy this role must tread on treacherously marshy ground. And the exercise of this role must consequently be accompanied by a certain caution and moderation.

The antibodies of the American social and political organism — aided by the new communications technology which proved its value so impressively during the televised Army-McCarthy hearings — are already powerfully at work. They may be trusted to contain and eventually to eliminate the demagogue from Wisconsin.

7. The Real Issue:
How to Combat Communism Responsibly

Communism on its way to power fosters disorder, internal divisions, and the confusion of issues. So does Senator McCarthy. This is not to suggest that McCarthy is a secret Communist (a characterization he himself does not hesitate to apply to others). What we *do* suggest is that the methods he uses to get to power are similar to those used by the Communists.

Two years ago Herbert Philbrick, the highest-placed FBI counterspy yet to be publicly identified, emerged from the Communist underground. An editorial in *The Christian Science Monitor,* based on an interview with Philbrick, reported:

> . . . And, says he [Philbrick], the hard-bitten Communist elite "just love" Senator McCarthy's name-calling because (1) it creates confusion, (2) it makes their party's strength seem much bigger than it really is, and (3) it greatly harms those whom the comrades call "those stupid liberals."

Perhaps the chief damage resulting from the controversy over the Senator's activities is that genuine anti-Communists have allowed themselves to be set at odds — in attacking and in defending McCarthy. They have thus been diverted from the serious business of fighting Communist subversion at home and Communist aggression abroad — two aspects of a single struggle that cannot safely be disjoined.[1]

[1] It is illusory to make a sharp separation between the internal danger of Communist subversion and the external threat of Soviet imperialism. To be sure, the principal threat is the Soviet Union's aggressive intent backed by its military potential, and the danger from native Communists would be negligible without it. But it must be remembered that American Communists have voluntarily and consciously submitted to the discipline, and have put themselves at the disposal, of an international conspiracy that has used any method to achieve its imperialist aims, from outright conquest (e.g., the Baltic states) to the internal destruction of a democratic nation (e.g., Czechoslovakia).

The effect, if not the intent, of McCarthy's activities has been to polarize the democratic community. At one extreme are those sincere anti-Communists who declare or imply that anyone or anything attacked by McCarthy is, *ipso facto,* to be considered suspect or guilty and deserving of denunciation, and that anyone who criticizes McCarthy is playing into the hands of the Communists.

At the other extreme are those equally sincere anti-Communists who declare or imply that anyone or anything attacked by McCarthy is, *ipso facto,* to be considered sacrosanct, innocent, and worthy of defense.

Both are emotional attitudes. Neither is warranted by the facts. Both are dependent on McCarthy as a guide to their own behavior. Both attitudes serve to foster a division around a false issue — a division of the libertarian forces that should be united in the defense of this country and of the cause of freedom. And perhaps the greatest danger implicit in this division is that it plays directly into the hands of the Communists — whose current tactic is to exploit this division as part of their long-range strategy of obscuring the real issues and destroying the anti-Communist unity of the American people.

As this book has tried to show, Senator McCarthy's attacks have been so consistently wide of the mark that we are obliged to evaluate them in general, not as justified or unjustified, but as irrelevant. Little, either good or bad, may be concluded about the object of a McCarthy attack from the *fact* that McCarthy *has* attacked. But, as we have seen, a great deal may be concluded as to the damaging nature of the Senator's impact on the government and on the country as a whole.

We have said nothing specifically about How To Fight Mc-Carthyism because we believe, very simply, that the only way to counter the effects of a lie is to present the truth, to set the record straight. This we have tried to do.

But in seeking to clear the air and set the record straight we believe it is valuable to state explicitly How *Not* To Fight Mc-Carthyism:

1. Don't fight McCarthy with his own methods

To do so would amount to participation in the very evil that one opposes. This would only aggravate the currently polarized political situation and could lead, in the course of a battle between half-truths and falsehoods, to the degeneration of moral standards in political debate and controversy.

Furthermore the Senator, one of the shrewdest in-fighters ever to appear on the American political scene, likes nothing better than to have his opponents meet him on his own ground and with his own weapons. Under such circumstances he stands to gain more than he loses.[2]

For example, we consider Senator Flanders' barely camouflaged insinuations about the personal relations of McCarthy and Cohn and Schine harmful, for two reasons: (a) such charges or innuendoes, carrying with them scandalous connotations, should not be made in public except in the context of official reports incorporating incontrovertible evidence; (b) the difficulty of proving allegations of this kind impairs the validity of the political criticism with which they are associated.

2. Don't exaggerate McCarthy's power and influence; don't be taken in by his bluff

The Senator is both less clever than he thinks and less reckless than he seems to many others.

The danger implicit in exaggeration is threefold: (a) it prevents a realistic assessment of the political situation, which is the first prerequisite to effective action; (b) it gives rise to reactions of hysteria and fear which may paralyze effective action; (c) it cuts the ground of common understanding from under libertarians, conservative and liberal, who would otherwise unite both to counter McCarthyism and to combat the greater evil of Communism.

For a responsible citizenry, what is the alternative to McCarthyism? How can we guarantee the internal and external security of our country — which McCarthy has failed to do — and do it with the least possible infringement of the freedom and security of the individual citizen?

The basic problem breaks down into these components:

— What are the requirements of an effective, non-political government security program designed to detect and eliminate *real*, not *imaginary*, security risks? What prerogatives, if any, should the government employee enjoy within such a program?

---

[2] On June 16, 1954, Assistant Secretary of Defense H. Struve Hensel swore that Senator McCarthy had told him that McCarthy follows a maxim taught him by an Indian named "Charlie" with whom he had once worked on a farm. Charlie, according to Senator McCarthy, urged the rule that "if one was ever approached by another person in a not completely friendly fashion, one should start kicking at the other person as fast as possible below the belt until the other person was rendered helpless."

— What should be the role of Congressional committees in the development and maintenance of such a program?

— How far must security measures be extended into private industry? What must be the relation between national security and job security in industry? How should our schools and colleges cope with the problem of Communist faculty members, while still maintaining in full force the principle of academic freedom?

— What are the requirements of an immigration policy designed both to keep out Communist spies and diversionists and also to encourage the admission of anti-totalitarian refugees and the defection of Communists from Iron Curtain countries — especially political and military leaders, scientists, and skilled professional persons?

— What is the proper role of civic groups, private organizations, and individuals in the maintenance of security against subversion, and in positive programs of education about the nature, goals, and methods of Communism and other forms of totalitarianism?

— What are the obligations of the individual citizen to the security program and to the government agencies (including Congressional committees) by which it is administered, enforced, or investigated?

Understanding Communism

A good officer doesn't send his troops into battle until he has what in Army jargon is called "an estimate of the situation." This includes all the available knowledge about the enemy. Fortunately, in the case of Communism the information is available — but deplorably little of it is known to many of those who would oppose Communism.

A careful distinction has to be drawn between teaching Communism and teaching *about* Communism. The first must be opposed, but the second is the indispensable first step toward creating a widespread understanding of who the enemy is, of what his avowed and his real goals are, of how he operates.

Americans need to know about the ideas of Marx; the basic theory and strategy of Communism; the extent to which these ideas have influenced European and Asian intellectuals; the tactics used by Communist agitators and propagandists to gain power. The critical study of such information in schools and in the media of popular communication should, in fact, be encouraged, rather than feared, as a necessary form of anti-Communist education.

The Voice of America and other government information agencies give daily accounts of Communism to their audiences abroad; but they do not help Americans in *their* understanding of the subject. It is incumbent upon privately controlled media to enlighten the American people on a subject about which, every test shows, they are grossly ignorant. Civic groups and private organizations of all kinds must find important roles to play in such an organized and systematic utilization of our educational resources and our communications industries.

For example, radio, television, and movies can all be effective; but they are not effective when they depict Communism merely as a cops-and-robbers story, or Stalinism merely as a roughly defined bogey with a shape but no substance. The American people have shown a taste for fine documentary films, and there is no subject more suitable to this intrinsically dramatic technique than Communism. The programs should be prepared under the guidance not only of television or moving-picture experts but also of persons grounded in a knowledge of Communist history, strategy, motives, and techniques. These may have to be coaxed out of their libraries or ivory towers — but they could and should be persuaded to join in what would be one of the most important educational tasks of our time.

The mass-communications media would provide the most dramatic means for implementing this educational program. But the basic means of acquiring knowledge is still the printed word. Valuable books dealing with Communism are available.[3]

School boards, church organizations, educational groups, and foundations might take the initiative in increasing the amount of accurate, factual — and interesting — materials available to the public. No one should have to read a dull work on a subject that is provocative.

The co-operation of large-circulation magazines and newspapers would be especially helpful. The nation would take a tremendous step in public education if nearly every newspaper ran a short, elementary series on the facts about Communism, written in lucid but not oversimplified language by men who know the field.

[3] Among several basic primers is *The Rise of Modern Communism* by Massimo Salvadori (New York: Holt, 1952; 118 pp.). An introduction on an intermediate level is *Bolshevism: An Introduction to Soviet Communism* by Waldemar Gurian (University of Notre Dame Press, 1952; 189 pp.). More advanced, more difficult — but more rewarding — books include *Three Who Made a Revolution* by Bertram D. Wolfe (New York: John Day, 1948; 661 pp.) and *Sociology and Psychology of Communism* by Jules Monnerot (Boston: Beacon, 1953; 339 pp.).

The more widely Communism is understood, the better able Americans will be to take — or to urge their elected representatives to take — the steps outlined in the following pages.

I. LOYALTY AND SECURITY
IN GOVERNMENT SERVICE

The history of the past ten years has demonstrated conclusively the need for a comprehensive, rational, and effective government security program. The revelations of Igor Gouzenko, Walter Krivitsky, Whittaker Chambers, and Elizabeth Bentley, leading to the discovery of Communist espionage rings involving such agents as Alger Hiss, Klaus Fuchs, and the Rosenbergs, leave no doubt as to the insidious and ever-present threat posed by Communist infiltration of the government. A security program must embody procedures that will protect the interests of the United States by making it as unlikely as possible for subversives to cause damage.

The basic principle of such a program must be that government employment is not a right but a privilege. The interests of national security must take indisputable precedence. And in cases where the interests of the employee and the government *cannot reasonably be reconciled,* the interests of the entire American people as represented by their government must be the primary consideration.

This does not mean that the interests of the employee should be ignored. On the contrary, the employee should be given every legitimate consideration, for three elementary reasons: (a) it is to the interest of the government itself to maintain and improve the morale, efficiency, and quality of a non-political Civil Service; (b) the employee's interests include such fundamental things as his job, his earning power, and his reputation, and he must not be lightly deprived of these; and (c) consideration for the employee's interests is a fundamental aspect of democratic standards of fairness and decency.

But the employee has no inherent right to a government job — and his interests must give way if they conflict with the interests of national security.

It must be recognized immediately, however, that there can be no such thing as *absolute* security. Even totalitarian states have failed to attain that impossible goal, and a democratic state would destroy itself and its citizens if it sought to achieve *absolute* security. Man is not infallible; human and social life are inevitably subject to risk, bad judgment, and failure, and these are condemned as crimes only in totalitarian societies. The purpose of a security program in a democracy must be to minimize as much as possible both the chance and the consequences of failure. But such a program must be flexible enough to allow for human redemption, to make it possible for an individual to repair his mistakes and continue to render service to the nation.

This principle was formulated perfectly by Thomas E. Murray, when he joined three of his four colleagues on the Atomic Energy Commission, on June 29, 1954, in passing an adverse judgment on the security status of atomic scientist J. Robert Oppenheimer. Although Murray did not apply the principle in this case, he stated:

> . . . it would be unwise, unjust and dangerous to admit that, as a principle, errors of judgment, especially in complicated situations, can furnish valid grounds for later indictments of a man's loyalty, character or status as a security risk. It has happened before in the long history of the United States that the national interests were damaged by errors of judgment committed by Americans in positions of responsibility. But these men did not for this reason cease to merit the trust of their country.

There are three basic categories into which a government security program must fall — loyalty, professional fitness, and security.

A. Loyalty

Clearly, a government security program should eliminate or prevent the employment of disloyal persons. But unrealistic reliance on the "loyalty" phase of a security program suffers from two serious defects. In the first place, it tends to damage the reputation and prospects of an employee who is under investigation — where all the facts are not yet in. More important, it is self-defeating: loyalty, in the absence of an overt act of disloyalty, is virtually impossible to identify, for it involves an assessment of subjective disposition and an evaluation of motives. (An overt act of disloyalty is, of course, a matter for the courts and not for administrative action.)

It was one of the grave drawbacks of the Truman administration's security program that it placed the major emphasis on finding grounds for doubting the loyalty of an employee. And it is one of the major advantages of the Eisenhower program that the loyalty and security programs are now formally combined. This means that decisions will tend to emphasize security, which can be ascertained with far more objectivity and accuracy than loyalty.

B. Professional Fitness

It would be senseless to appoint or keep in policy-making office an ardent protectionist to administer a free-trade policy, a real-estate lobbyist to administer a public-housing program, a firm advocate of private power to administer the TVA. And it would be equally senseless to appoint to the State Department a man — even though his loyalty and reliability might be unquestioned — who believed that State Department policies were wrong and dangerous. A man cannot be expected to carry out effectively a law or a program that he is likely to oppose.

Basic policies are formulated by a democratically elected administration to advance the national interests at it sees them. It must have the indisputable right to shift or remove employees who it has reason to believe might retard the execution of its policies. This is not the same as persecution of a man for his ideas. It is merely sane administration and a practical working out of the democratic process. Such a program becomes persecution only when an employee is removed or shifted from his post for ideas or associations that do not have a vital bearing on his assigned duties.

It should be a principle of government that, within the framework of a non-partisan career Civil Service, any administration has the right to dismiss from policy-making positions civil servants who are committed to a position basically incompatible with the administration's own policies. This principle has no relation to the man's loyalty, or even to his ability. In case of incompatibility in basic aims, the employee should either be dismissed or be moved to another government position where his status would remain protected, where his abilities could be utilized, and where his sympathies would not impede the implementation of policy.

C. Security

The bulk of cases handled under a government security program involve the determination of "security risks." Here much thought must be given to the formulation of standards and procedures both to protect national security and to insure fair disposition of the employee's case.

Probably everyone except Senator McCarthy and his most extreme supporters would be ready to agree that this nation, its government, and its law-enforcement agencies are by now adequately security-conscious. To assert this is not to suggest that there is no longer any need for a security program. As we have indicated, the threat of Communist infiltration and subversion is an unceasing one, and eternal vigilance is indispensable to our national safety.

But the problem today is no longer to alert the public and the government to this threat, or to establish a firm security program. The problem today is to correct and improve the existing program, whose over-zealous administration has resulted in numerous abuses and injustices (see Chapter 4). To cite just a few of the scores of cases that could be adduced:

(1) A well-known, conservative social scientist of the highest repute, always a Republican, discovered that his clearance for obtaining classified documents from the Defense Department had been suspended because he had "associated" with two other social scientists accused of being security risks. These other two men are not and never have been Communists, or even fellow-travelers.

(2) A well-known economist had his clearance suspended on the flimsiest of charges, based on contributions he had made to the Russian War Relief during World War II, and on courses taught by others at his university. This man was never a Communist or even a fellow-traveler.

(3) An important area study made for the Defense Department by a private research organization was scheduled to be circulated to eight top experts for their appraisal. Seven of these men could not get security clearance.

Such cases have arisen because (a) security regulations are vague; (b) many security officers, ill-informed as to the nature and history of Communism, are not equipped to evaluate an individual's past history with any understanding and discrimination; and (c) even well-qualified security officers are sometimes afraid to exercise the meager amount of initiative and judgment allowed them by the existing regulations and standards.

This state of affairs has frequently resulted in intolerable confusion and delay in the operation of sensitive departments and bureaus; in loss to the government of the services of able and loyal citizens who have never had any connection with the Communist conspiracy; in unjustified hardship and annoyance for scientists and scholars of the highest repute; and in some instances in a serious slowdown of defense operations.

The situation calls for the appointment of a special Presidential commission or a joint committee of Congress, armed with a comprehensive and explicit mandate to examine all aspects of the security problem. The new body should be asked to bring in recommendations for changes in existing security legislation and for standard procedures to be adopted by Congressional investigating committees. The tests and criteria to be applied by security administrators in both government and private industry where defense contracts are in force should be thoroughly examined.

The need for such a comprehensive study and report is manifest. Meanwhile it should be possible to remedy, by administrative order, some of the more obvious defects of the program.[4] Here are some of the steps that could be taken in short order:

1. A public restatement of security policy

This statement should be designed to restore the shaken morale of government workers, to promote public understanding of the problems involved, and to speed up the machinery of clearance.

2. The issuance of new directives to security officers

These directives should provide the security officers of all government departments with simplified and realistic criteria for the determination of security risks. The directives should clearly establish the critical distinctions between (a) espionage agents; (b) Communist Party members and affiliates, with or without Party cards; and (c) Communist fellow-travelers and sympathizers, as determined by membership in Communist-front organizations and especially by adherence to the Party line at critical periods such as that of the Stalin-Hitler pact.

Where evidence of past involvement is balanced by evidence of subsequent public repudiation of the Party and its fronts and by documented anti-Communist actions, the directives should provide for clearance at the discretion of the security officer and the department chief.

Evidence of membership in the Socialist Party and its affiliated organizations should be specifically excluded from the category of "derogatory information." Throughout the free world, socialists have been among the earliest and most effective opponents of

---

[4] A glaring defect of the present program was conceded, ironically enough, by R. W. Scott McLeod, State Department Security Officer, at an executive session of a House Appropriations subcommittee on January 25, 1954. Asked whether the Department's present security procedures would have uncovered a spy like Alger Hiss, McLeod replied that they would not have. The point is that no security program, no matter how stringent, will succeed in uncovering an espionage agent as deeply buried and entrenched as Hiss. Only the effective work of counter-intelligence or a defector like Whittaker Chambers or Elizabeth Bentley is likely to accomplish this.

totalitarianism, both Communist and Fascist. Democratic socialists were also the strongest and most persistent defenders of freedom in Russia before and after the Bolshevik Revolution — until their suppression.

3. The strengthening of security personnel

At all levels, only politically experienced people should be employed as security officers. This principle should not prevent the employment of former Communist Party members and sympathizers if their past experience equips them to understand and apply realistic criteria of loyalty and security, and if their subsequent anti-Communist activity has demonstrated their loyalty, reliability, and good judgment.

4. The realistic selection of categories of employment for which clearance is required

The vast majority of government employees do not occupy sensitive positions. The problem here is to determine which positions are "sensitive." Such a determination will always and inevitably involve certain risks, since human fallibility cannot provide for every conceivable contingency or for the ingenuity of an unusually clever infiltrator. Nevertheless, it is patent that "over-classification" of non-sensitive positions would overburden the already harried investigative agencies, would slow down their work enormously and thus interfere with the day-to-day operations of government, and would in the end result in a breakdown of the purposes of the security system by making it impossible to check thoroughly the reliability of employees in the really sensitive positions.

The classification of positions with respect to sensitivity should not be left in the hands of security officers, who have a vested professional interest in maximizing the sensitive categories. Such determinations should be made by a panel of independent experts operating as an autonomous arm of the Civil Service Commission. If independent experts classified sensitive and non-sensitive positions, they would undoubtedly be moved to decide — as a New York State court decided — that the possibility that a city-park washroom attendant might be a Communist would not necessarily constitute a grave threat to security. In this case the duties performed by the employee were taken as criteria relevant to the question of security.

5. The establishment of new standards for security hearings

This is perhaps the most difficult problem to settle. These hearings are not equivalent to a trial in a court of law: they are not set up to determine a man's guilt or innocence. Their function must not be to attempt to punish an unlawful or disloyal act. Standards of guilt are determined by the legislature and are implemented by the law-enforcement agencies and the courts.

The security-hearing panels are purely administrative boards set up with only one function: to elicit all the necessary information to enable a government department to determine whether an employee may or may not be reliable in a sensitive post.

The panel must have considerably wider latitude in considering information that would help it arrive at a determination than would pertain to the rules of evidence in a court of law.

Because an employee's innocence and guilt are not at stake in a security hearing, he does not have, on the basis of abstract principle, the right to invoke the principle of presumed innocence until guilt is proven — as would be the case in a court of law. In a concrete situation, however, the belief that the employee has the right to invoke the principle of presumed innocence is quite understandable. For too often, unfortunately, all the stigmata of presumed guilt instantly attach to a man against whom charges have been leveled, in or out of security channels. The invocation of the principle of presumed innocence is a natural reaction to the disadvantageous position into which the alleged security risk has been forced by an unfair public sentiment, too frequently exploited by politicians for partisan reasons.

When we argue that "innocence" and "guilt" are irrelevant to a security hearing, we recognize that the policy we advocate can operate fairly only within a context of enlightened public opinion and decent standards of political behavior; otherwise the principle becomes a travesty. If the employee is in fact judged and punished as though he had been found guilty of a crime, he could demand the courtroom right to maintain his innocence until proved guilty.

Within the context of this principle, the difference between a court trial and a security hearing is quite clear. In a court trial the accused is constitutionally protected from being forced to be a witness against himself and may therefore refuse to testify. Such failure to testify may not be used as an indication of guilt. But in a security hearing, where the relevant problem is not guilt but fitness for employment, the failure to answer pertinent questions must be taken into consideration by the employer — the government.

This principle is fundamental to any employment procedure, government or private, sensitive or non-sensitive. The government must have at least the same right in determining the reliability of an employee or a prospective employee as a businessman normally has in hiring a secretary — namely, the right to insist on an answer to pertinent questions.

Nevertheless the individual employee should be accorded every possible protection that would not frustrate the purposes of the security program. To deny that a man has certain legal rights in a security process does not mean that he should be deprived of the protections afforded by considerations of decency and fairness. An employee may not have a *legal right* to counsel in a government hearing — but he should in fairness be accorded that privilege. He may not have the *legal right* to be presented with a formal statement of charges — but he should be accorded that privilege too, so that he will not be operating in the dark and so that the security panel will not be tempted to take advantage of him.

In many cases an employee who has entered into security proceedings must temporarily have his clearance lifted for access to classified information — so as to minimize or eliminate danger to the national security. But it would seem unnecessary and unjust to suspend him from his job while his status is still indeterminate and while he needs whatever income he can get to organize and finance his defense. Consideration should be given also to the proposal that the employee be supplied with counsel if he does not have the means to retain one himself.

In addition, hearing boards ought to be composed of persons from outside the government, who will consequently not be subject to pressure from either the Executive or the Legislative Branch. It should not be difficult to find persons who combine a knowledge of Communism and security requirements with wisdom and common sense.

A case in point is the security-hearing panel that dealt with the charges against Dr. J. Robert Oppenheimer. There may be much to criticize both as to the security regulations within which the panel necessarily had to operate and as to the arguments and the decisions themselves. But from a purely procedural point of view the composition of that panel was admirably suited to the reform suggested here.

Finally, it might also be desirable to apply more generally the system in force at the Defense Department, which has set up specific standards for positions of varying degrees of sensitivity. A hearing board could then determine an employee's fitness for a given degree of sensitive position but not necessarily for a higher one. This kind of refinement in the security system could serve to keep in government service competent and loyal individuals who, under the circumstances of their particular jobs, would not be security risks at all.

Many anti-Communists, in and out of government, believe that a rationalization of the security program along some such lines would at once improve the morale of government workers, cut down the staggering backlog of delayed clearances that burdens many government establishments, and release FBI and other security personnel for the serious business of digging out deeply hidden Communist subversives and espionage agents.

II. THE ROLE OF CONGRESSIONAL COMMITTEES

In the development of an effective security program, the Legislative Branch has a legitimate and necessary role. Congressional investigating committees can serve a valuable function in developing facts, in educating public opinion, and in framing legislation. Too often, however, especially in the internal-security field, Congressional committees have been tempted to exploit rather than educate public sentiment, to seek publicity rather than constructive legislation and the revelation of facts. This has been especially true, as we have seen, of the investigations conducted by Senator McCarthy.

The Congressional role in this field needs rationalization just as much as the administrative procedures. For example, there are three separate Congressional committees engaged in security investigations. One is of course McCarthy's Permanent Subcommittee on Investigations. The other two groups have on occasion performed valuable services — notably, the Senate Internal Security Subcommittee (formerly headed by Pat McCarran and subsequently by William Jenner), which produced the facts on the Institute of Pacific Relations; and the House Committee on Un-American Activities (headed by Harold Velde), which under an earlier chairman elicited the valuable testimony of Whittaker Chambers and Elizabeth Bentley.

Not infrequently, however, these committees have exceeded the bounds of fairness, of decency — and of accuracy. Often they have competed for publicity and duplicated one another's efforts. For example, the Jenner and Velde groups conducted concurrent investigations of subversion in the schools and colleges, and certain witnesses appeared before both committees.

Numerous suggestions for rationalization have been proposed, notably in the bills introduced by Independent Senator Morse and Democratic Senator Kefauver, and by Republican Representatives Keating and Javits. This legislation would subject Congressional committees to procedural rules designed to minimize publicity-hunting, to prevent abuse of innocent persons, and to speed up the machinery of the inquiries. Congressman Javits has urged that responsibility for the investigation of Communist infiltration be concentrated in a single joint committee similar to the Joint Congressional Atomic Energy Committee, which conducts its activities with quiet efficiency.

What about the "Fifth Amendment Communists" who have appeared before Congressional committees? The Fifth Amendment to the Constitution provides that "no witness . . . shall be compelled in any criminal case to be a witness against himself . . ." This has been interpreted by the courts to signify that a witness may refuse to answer questions that he believes may tend to incriminate him at some future time, and it has been further interpreted to apply to Congressional hearings as well as criminal proceedings.

It should not be automatically assumed that all such silent witnesses are Communists or pro-Communists. On the other hand, those who invoke the Fifth Amendment, and suffer economic or social penalties in consequence, should not be automatically regarded as heroes or martyrs unless their reasons for silence or non-cooperation are known. Among those who have left the Party are many who are still sympathetic enough to it to give it the protection of secrecy.

In addition to the many active Communists who have invoked this constitutional privilege, there have been a few ex-Communists and former fellow-travelers who have never openly repudiated the Communist conspiracy. In answering questionnaires and in taking loyalty oaths, they may have unwisely chosen to conceal their previous Communist affiliations or sympathies; they therefore fear (with some reason) that frank testimony about their past may subject them to perjury indictments, affect adversely their present reformed status, and perhaps jeopardize friends and associates with similar pasts.

In addition a number of non-Communist liberals have attempted to use the Fifth Amendment privilege to express a conscientious objection to some or all of the current Congressional investigations of Communism.

In evaluating the testimony of these various categories of witnesses, one must avoid incriminating the innocent along with the guilty, the principled libertarian along with the disciplined totalitarian.

However, it remains true that the non-Communist witness who refuses information to a Congressional committee or a government agency on the ground that it will tend to incriminate him places a shadow on his own reputation. He also fails to accomplish the purpose of his silence, if his purpose is to protest effectively against the nature and methods of the particular inquiry.

By contrast, the position taken by those who have chosen to defend civil liberties before Congressional committees not by silence, but by free and sometimes eloquent speech, has proved far more effective. This was the position of Granville Hicks, a distinguished literary critic and staunch anti-Communist, who in 1953 testified before the House Committee on Un-American Activities concerning his early Communist years. He gave the committee full and frank information about his own record and that of former associates of whom he had direct personal knowledge. But he went on to make the excellent point that investigating committees should concern themselves not only with how much Communism there is, but also with how little. For example, he suggested that it would help to dispel public fears if it were realized that there were only fourteen Communists at Harvard University in 1940 and perhaps only one at the time of the committee's inquiry.

Should a witness testify frankly not only about his own past as a Communist or fellow-traveler but about that of his friends and associates as well?

The question poses delicate considerations of personal honor and responsibility. But it would seem to be the part of wisdom as well as of courage to answer it affirmatively. Speaking out fully and frankly serves to establish the credibility of the witness. It is probably also the best method of vindicating one's own values.

The Communist Party has profited greatly by the reluctance of liberals to be considered "red-baiters." Conversely, a former Communist who testifies frankly about his past associations often thereby helps to expose dangerous current activities of the Party.

Frank testimony of this sort does not make one an "informer," with all the distasteful connotations of that word. On the contrary, if a silent witness must be protected in his right to invoke the Fifth Amendment, a forthright witness must be equally protected from slanderous insinuations against his reputation and idealism. The man who testifies frankly about the past Communist record of former friends and associates performs the same public service as the witness who testifies to his personal knowledge of the past Nazi or Fascist record of former friends and associates.

Both may be patriots who place the highest value on the safety of their countrymen. They may be persons who believe so deeply in the value of freedom and democracy that they will sacrifice the comfort of their own silence and the emotional ties of personal attachment to the ideals they honor.

III. LOYALTY AND SECURITY IN PRIVATE EMPLOYMENT

A. Industry

In many industries, especially those engaged in contract work for the armed services, the danger of Communist infiltration and espionage is as serious as in sensitive government departments. But here too there has been much waste and slowdown as a result of vague loyalty-and-security criteria applied by timid or poorly qualified security officers. Here too a rationalization of security procedures is in order.

Government, rather than industry, should determine the sectors of private industry that are in fact highly sensitive defense areas. The methods for protecting security in these sectors should be the same as those employed in government. If security processes are extended beyond these sectors, there is a danger that private industries might develop over-elaborate investigative departments that could easily become labor spy systems.

It should be possible to secure the co-operation of government, management, and the labor-union movement (which is overwhelmingly anti-Communist) in formulating and implementing an effective security system for sensitive private industries.

B. Communications Media

Aside from the sensitive sectors of private industry, the areas where Communist infiltration are potentially most dangerous are in the communications media and in education. In both fields an intelligent anti-Communist policy is called for — and in fact is slowly being evolved.

Communist infiltration of all the communications media has in the past unquestionably placed Party members and sympathizers in key positions which they used in an attempt to condition American public opinion favorably to Communist objectives. It need only be pointed out, for example, how difficult it was just a few years ago to publish in leading newspaper book-review sections unfavorable reviews of books that reflected the Lattimore position on Far Eastern policy. Communists in key positions in radio and television frequently prevented the employment of their political opponents.

The pendulum has now swung the other way — to such an extent that many injustices have been done. A listing in *Red Channels* of the names of radio and television artists may not be legally libelous against a political innocent, but it has frequently resulted in unjust employment discrimination. Broadcasters and advertisers clearly have a right to employ whomever they choose; they have a right *not* to hire entertainers whom they believe to be Communists. But they must be severely censured for the panicky dismissal of artists merely because their inclusion in *Red Channels* has made them "controversial figures."

Actually the number of active Communists in the entertainment field is today minute; it provides a striking contrast with the much larger number of political innocents and people whose connections with Communist fronts have been transitory and tenuous. The situation calls for a kind of informal "statute of limitations" within the entertainment industry, for people whose past activities are fully balanced by their subsequent repudiation of Communism and all its works.

The object of such a procedure would be to take innocent or innocuous people "off the hook" and to improve the morale of the professions concerned. A "clearance" program has in fact been initiated by the television industry, although the machinery of its operation still leaves something to be desired.

C. Education

In regard to education two important points must be made. In the first place, the number of Communist teachers in public schools and universities is today infinitesimal, and those that remain are being effectively routed, chiefly by school boards operating quietly and fairly. This fact is attested to by all the investigating agencies, including Congressional committees, that have looked into the problem.

Secondly, the vast majority of teachers have accepted the principle that members of a totalitarian conspiracy cannot be expected to respect the ethical canons of the teaching profession. Hence current membership in the Communist Party should be regarded as *prima facie* evidence of their unfitness to teach. This principle has been accepted in a variety of formulations by the official organizations of the American teaching profession.

It has been suggested that legal acknowledgment of this principle might end the debate about the "right" of such persons to teach. And it could provide a substitute for the futile and humiliating verbal incantations to which teachers must subject themselves when they sign loyalty oaths.

As for teachers who adhere to the Party line but cannot be shown to be Party members, the overwhelming majority of teachers agree that the faculties themselves are the best judges of fitness to teach. There are exceptionally few of this type also. And each case should be judged individually by professional colleagues in terms of the generally accepted principles of academic competence and fitness to teach.

IV. SECURITY AND AMERICAN IMMIGRATION POLICY

Our immigration laws and their administration must be designed to prevent the admission of Communist agents into this country. American immigration policy — especially as it affects potential defectors from Iron Curtain countries — must also play an important role in the resistance of free peoples to Communist aggression. Communist propaganda has made capital of our failure to deal intelligently and generously with these potential recruits to the cause of freedom. And our friends in the free world have been seriously disquieted by the overly restrictive nature of procedures that have barred distinguished visitors and nameless others from entry into this country.

The Internal Security Act of 1950 embodied sweeping provisions barring from American shores anarchists, Communists, Fascists, and members of organizations advocating totalitarian doctrines. It also banned the immigration of persons advocating the use of sabotage or assassination of officials of any organized government. This latter provision could easily be interpreted to exclude militant anti-Communists from Iron Curtain countries who would not be reluctant to use force to rid their native countries of Communist tyrants.

In administering the act, the Immigration Service at first went beyond the purposes of its authors. For example, membership in Fascist trade unions and other organizations, to which all citizens of Hitler's Germany and Mussolini's Italy were forced to belong, was interpreted as disqualifying an individual for admission to the United States.

In June 1952, the earlier law was superseded by the present McCarran-Walter Act. Under its provisions, persons are exempt from the ban if they were members of totalitarian groups when they were under sixteen years of age, or had joined solely to obtain food, employment, or other essentials of life.

But Section 212 of the Act bars "aliens who the consular officer or the Attorney General knows or has reason to believe seek to enter the United States solely, principally, or incidentally to engage in activities which would be prejudicial to the public interest or endanger the welfare, safety or security of the United States." This provision has at least two serious drawbacks: (a) prospective immigrants are forced to go through interminable red tape in order to obtain the approval of both the consular authorities abroad and the immigration authorities in the United States; and (b) there is no definition of what constitutes "activities . . . prejudicial to the public interest. . . ." Consular and immigration authorities have frequently made arbitrary and haphazard rulings that have been both ludicrous and unjust.

One of the most objectionable provisions of the law requires the deportation of any alien who at any time after admission has been active in Communist or totalitarian political causes — regardless of whether such activities were clearly a mistake, the mistake acknowledged, and the association terminated. Another section requires deportation of any alien who was once associated with activities "prejudicial to the public interest," even if such activities had long since ceased or such associations had been innocently made.

These and other objectionable features of the law were sharply criticized during the 1952 election campaign by both Dwight D. Eisenhower and Adlai Stevenson. Nevertheless, the law remains on the books — in spite of its demonstrated harmfulness both in keeping out people who are basically on our side, and in lowering American prestige abroad.

The McCarran Act cost former Italian Premier de Gasperi's center coalition heavily in the Italian elections of 1953. Both the quota system, which discriminated against Italian immigration, and the resentment felt by non-Communist and anti-Communist Italians who found themselves prevented from immigration to this country by the security provisions of the McCarran law, played a role in this situation.

Moreover, the requirement that the security status of sailors in foreign merchant fleets be checked before the sailors were allowed shore leave in the United States compounded a series of egregious blunders. The new regulation countered an old tradition that had long protected the status of sailors in foreign ports; it outraged the sensibilities and national pride of our sea-faring French, British, and Scandinavian friends; and its simpleminded procedures could have no effect on the operations of a clever Communist intelligence and underground network.

The attendance of a few Communist scientists or scholars at an international conference could scarcely hurt this country as much as the decision of an international professional organization to refrain from meeting here in the future because of the restrictions of the McCarran Act. The inconsistency of the law is illustrated by the admission of Russian chess players while a few Communist scholars and visitors are shut out.

The development of an immigration policy that will help, not hurt, our side in the Cold War should be an important objective for all anti-Communists.

V. THE ROLE OF PRIVATE ORGANIZATIONS

Civic groups and other private organizations that concern themselves with aiding the struggle against totalitarianism can be exceedingly helpful — or dangerous.

When the American Legion took a vigorous stand against the forcible repatriation of North Korean and Chinese war prisoners, at a moment when the State Department was reported to be wavering on the principle, the Legion struck a blow for freedom the importance of which can scarcely be exaggerated.

On the other hand, when veterans and other civic groups take it upon themselves to censor forum speakers, judge the political correctness of school textbooks, and evaluate the loyalty of persons suspected of being Communists, they go beyond their proper functions and do a disservice to the cause of freedom.[5]

Civic groups can play an important and constructive role in exposing falsehoods spread by Communists, and in removing the illusions of the politically naive who have been duped by the plausible prospectuses of Communist-front organizations. But when such groups try to impose their own standards on their fellows by means outside the law, or in fields that the law does not reach, there is an obvious threat to traditional American liberties.

Above all, civic groups can serve as a major vehicle for the mass public-information program which is the indispensable foundation for an effective and constructive defense of freedom against Communist infiltration and subversion and against all other non-democratic manifestations in this country. They can help to clear up misunderstanding and misinformation and to implement a sound, democratic program to protect the security of government, industry, education, and every other important sector of our public life.

VI. IN CONCLUSION: A COMMENT ON THE
ETHICS OF CONTROVERSY

On March 4, 1954, the members of the American Committee for Cultural Freedom, aroused by the deplorable level of political discourse in the country, issued a public statement which concluded with a ten-point code of ethics for political discussion.[6] The code evidently filled a need, for it was widely quoted, reprinted, and discussed on radio stations, in newspapers and magazines, and on the floor of both houses of Congress.

In writing this book, we have tried to obey the edicts of this ten-point guide. We would want to be judged by this code, just as we believe it to be useful in judging the political behavior of others — including Senator McCarthy, the Communists, and the fellow-travelers of both.

[5] In Huntington (West Virginia), Salina (Kansas), and elsewhere, American Legion posts have interfered with the appearance of liberal speakers on public forums. In Phoenix (Arizona), the local Legion post denounced a college textbook written by reputable American scholars and used by the local Junior College. In Norwalk (Connecticut), publicity connected with the recruitment program of the local VFW post gave the community reason to fear a "witch-hunt," which never actually developed, however.

[6] The distinguished author of the code was Professor Sidney Hook, chairman of the Department of Philosophy at New York University, and a skilled political debater in his own right.

These are the ten points by which we think all political controversy ought to be guided:

(1) Nothing and no one is immune from criticism.

(2) Everyone involved in a controversy has an intellectual responsibility to inform himself of the available facts.

(3) Criticism should be directed first to policies, and against persons only when they are responsible for policies, and against their motives or purposes only when there is some independent evidence of their character.

(4) Because certain words are legally permissible, they are not therefore morally permissible.

(5) Before impugning an opponent's motives, even when they legitimately may be impugned, answer his arguments.

(6) Do not treat an opponent of a policy as if he were therefore a personal enemy, or an enemy of the country, or a concealed enemy of democracy.

(7) Since a good cause may be defended by bad arguments, after answering the bad arguments for another's position, present positive evidence for your own.

(8) Do not hesitate to admit lack of knowledge or to suspend judgment if evidence is not decisive either way.

(9) Because something is logically possible, it is not therefore probable. "It is not impossible" is a preface to an irrelevant statement about human affairs. The question is always one of the balance of probabilities.

(10) The cardinal sin, when we are looking for truth of fact or wisdom of policy, is refusal to discuss, or action which blocks discussion.

This book needs no peroration for an ending. Public responsibility required that a job of research and analysis be done. We have tried to do it in a way for which we could answer to American public opinion, to friendly foreign observers of the American political scene, and to our own consciences.

McCarthy's Discovery of Anti-Communism

The most impressive defense of Senator McCarthy appears in the documented study *McCarthy and His Enemies* by William F. Buckley, Jr., and L. Brent Bozell. Their book deals with McCarthy's anti-Communist crusade in the period from February 1950 to January 1953. In at least thirty places in the Buckley-Bozell book, the authors concede that the Senator has frequently resorted to inaccuracies, distortions, exaggerations, and falsehoods. As we have demonstrated in this book, which deals primarily with McCarthy in power *after* January 1953, the techniques of the Senator to which Buckley and Bozell refer — and which they deplore — were not accidental products of circumstances in which the Senator has found himself at various times in his career. They are, rather, characteristic of the man's political behavior, and they have flowered during his period in power.

While Buckley and Bozell do not find McCarthy's behavior above reproach, they excuse it on the following grounds:

(a) that Senator McCarthy intervened in the anti-Communist fight at the decisive moment, in 1950, when the evolution of public sentiment "from pro-Communism in the direction of anti-Communism seemed to have ground to a halt . . ." and that his intervention was the key factor in reviving public consciousness of the Communist threat;

(b) that McCarthy intervened in the decisive area of the anti-Communist fight — namely, infiltration, subversion, and espionage;

(c) that McCarthy's sincerity and effectiveness outweigh the questionable techniques he uses to get results.

All three arguments are open to serious question. There is no doubt that the Senator did point to a lax government security situation, and that his activities contributed to the tightening of security procedures and the elimination of a few actual or potential security risks. The foregoing chapters have already made clear the cost at which these accomplishments were bought, and Buckley and Bozell's justifications of the expense are not persuasive.

Let us examine each of them.

A. The "Decisive Moment" Excuse

The year 1950 — the year in which McCarthy entered the scene as an anti-Communist champion — cannot in any sense be considered a decisive one in the fight against the international Communist conspiracy.

First, infiltration, subversion, and espionage, by all available evidence, had been most widespread and most serious in the 1930's and 1940's (for example, Alger Hiss, Klaus Fuchs, the Rosenbergs). These were the periods of the United Front and of the Grand Alliance, when security measures against Communists were practically non-existent.

Second, the anti-Communist consciousness of the American people grew steadily between the end of World War II and 1950. Such events as the fall of China, the Berlin blockade, the Hiss case, the Communist coup in Czechoslovakia and the murder of Jan Masaryk, the Gouzenko case in Canada, the Fuchs case in England, the Judy Coplon case, the trial of the eleven top American Communist leaders, the leap to freedom of the Russian schoolteacher Kasenkina from the Soviet Consulate in New York, the revelations about Soviet espionage and slave-labor camps by Victor Kravchenko and others — all these contributed greatly to the general awakening of the American public (and their government) to the true nature of the Soviet system.

Third, the Communist attack on South Korea and the subsequent intervention of Red China in the Korean War — in 1950 — had a far greater impact on the progress of anti-Communist consciousness than anything McCarthy could have done or did do.

B. *The "Decisive Area" Excuse*

The problem of Communist infiltration and subversion in the United States is of course an important problem where it exists; but it does not represent the "most decisive area" of the anti-Communist front.

Buckley and Bozell attempt to justify Senator McCarthy's sole concentration on subversion and espionage by stating that ". . . conceivably a single individual could shift the balance of power by delivering to the Soviet Union technological secrets through the use of which they could overcome their strategic disadvantage and proceed to communize Europe." Yet this is a gross oversimplification. The balance of power is in the free world's favor not because of any significant technological secrets that we now possess. Our strength lies more in the strategy of our foreign policy, in our ideological appeal to the countries still free, in our efforts to strengthen through military security and social-economic reform and collective effort the non-Communist nations of the world. The importance of technological secrets may once have been great; but the Soviet Union has had our atomic secrets for many years and possesses the hydrogen bomb. Even without the advantages of espionage, Soviet scientists have moved far in developing weapons. (McCarthy did nothing — and of course was unable to do anything — to prevent such secrets from falling into Russian hands.) It is not because of technological weakness that the Russians have failed to communize western Europe; this they could accomplish only by war, and they have thus far been unwilling to risk an atomic war.

Since the World War II espionage of Rosenberg and Fuchs, no new cases of espionage have been revealed; where they exist the FBI and other government counter-espionage agencies are far more effective in uncovering and outmaneuvering them than any Congressional investigating subcommittee, no matter how conscientious. Moreover the FBI and the Central Intelligence Agency realize that spies are not foolish enough to expose themselves by belonging to Communist Party cells or to pro-Communist groups, or by giving themselves continuing records of Communist political activity.

McCarthy has not uncovered a single Russian spy. Spies are discovered by skilled counter-intelligence or by the defection of espionage agents like Chambers and Bentley. Congressional committees, as in the Hiss case, may be instrumental in forcing effective action against the spies.

Effective efforts to combat infiltration and subversion are indeed important for the defense of America and the rest of the free world. But they are not the only important areas of combat — and not the *most* important. Communism is a global conspiracy centered in Moscow; while American Communists are certainly dangerous, they are a threat primarily because of the gigantic military and industrial power for which they act as agents and apologists. There is little chance that American Communists can succeed in overthrowing the government in this country, where democracy is strong and stable; but there is considerable possibility that Soviet Communism, through imperialistic adventures and control of satellite states, could overthrow and dominate the governments of many free nations.

It is this threat to which sincere and informed anti-Communists direct their major efforts. McCarthy, however, has failed to show much concern for this threat. Among the Communist victories that have since 1950 advanced their strategy throughout the world, not one could have been prevented merely by a domestic crusade to rid the American scene of subversives (even had the crusade proved successful). And no serious roadblock, surely, is put in the way of the Communist conspiracy, either at home or abroad, by such slipshod and irresponsible efforts as those of Senator McCarthy.

C. The "Sincerity and Effectiveness" Excuse

The "effectiveness" of Senator McCarthy's crusade has already been dealt with in Chapter 4 above.

Whether McCarthy is "sincere" is difficult for an outsider to determine. Not even Buckley and Bozell can probe the mind of the junior Senator from Wisconsin. The judgment as to Senator McCarthy's sincerity must be based on an examination of his record.

McCarthy was elected to the Senate in 1946, as the result of a successful campaign against the incumbent Senator from Wisconsin, Robert La Follette, Jr. La Follette had been an extraordinarily effective anti-Communist legislator. His clear, forthright opposition to Roosevelt policies at Casablanca, Teheran, and Yalta, unlike that of some other Congressmen of the time, could not be and was not attacked by the Roosevelt supporters as stemming from a reactionary, isolationist position. For Senator La Follette was no longer an isolationist (as his father had been) and was among the most liberal members of Congress. Indeed, his combination of liberalism and anti-Communism, both effective, made him hated by the Communists.

But McCarthy accepted the support of the Communists in his campaign to defeat La Follette, arch-enemy of Communism.

Once in the Senate, McCarthy maintained a silence about the great historical developments that were educating the American people in the critical post-war period. No speech of any significance came from Senator McCarthy about the increasingly bitter struggle between the free world and Communism. In his first years in the Senate, when the free world was probably in greater danger than it is now or than it was at the time of the Wheeling speech,[1] McCarthy was a silent follower of the Republican Congressional leadership: moderately internationalist, a follower of the bi-partisan foreign policy in the manner of Harold Stassen.[2] McCarthy was not then allied with the group of militant, dedicated anti-Communists in the Senate, which included McCarran, Bridges, Wherry, and Eastland. These men were conservative; some of them were isolationists who opposed constructive measures like the Marshall Plan designed to strengthen the free world. But they had the virtue of being strongly anti-Communist and anti-Soviet in the critical years immediately following World War II. McCarthy did not join this group until much later. From 1947 until his new-found career as a militant anti-Communist, McCarthy's votes on major issues of foreign policy were in line with normative Republican voting:

In 1947 Senator McCarthy
> voted in favor of the Greek-Turkish military and economic aid bill;
> paired against an amendment to reduce interim foreign aid from $597,000,000 to $400,000,000;
> voted in favor of an amendment to increase foreign relief from $200,000,000 to $350,000,000.

In 1948 Senator McCarthy
> voted in favor of the European Recovery Program (Marshall Plan) to grant economic aid to free nations;
> voted in favor of the peacetime military draft;
> paired in favor of the bill to admit 202,000 displaced persons to the United States over a two-year period.

In 1949 Senator McCarthy
> voted against a 10 per cent cut in Marshall Plan funds;
> voted in favor of ratifying the North Atlantic Pact;
> introduced a resolution calling for a federal convention of delegates from the twelve sponsoring nations of NATO;
> voted in favor of extending the reciprocal trade-agreements program (for two instead of three years);
> voted in favor of the Mutual Defense Assistance Act authorizing aid to the NATO allies; *but*
> voted in favor of amendments to cut the actual Mutual Assistance appropriations by $200,000,000 and $100,000,000.

[1] In 1946 we had demobilized, the Soviets had not; we had pulled out of Europe, the Soviets had not.
[2] McCarthy was an important leader of the Stassen forces in the 1948 Republican Presidential primary election in Wisconsin, in opposition to the candidacy of General Douglas MacArthur. Similarly, at the 1948 Republican Convention he supported Stassen against General MacArthur.

Very suddenly, in 1950, McCarthy's record began to undergo a dramatic change. After he had found a promising method for increasing his power in the nation as an anti-Communist crusader, McCarthy moved into the circle of the isolationist, "nationalist" wing of the Republican Party from which he could get the strongest support. In precisely the period when the majority of the Republican Party was moving toward a substantially internationalist position, McCarthy was shifting toward the "new nationalist" side. Here is the record of his votes on major issues of foreign policy and of the world-wide anti-Communist fight from 1950 to 1953.[3]

In 1950 Senator McCarthy

> voted against the Point Four program to aid underdeveloped nations;
> voted against additional appropriations for the Voice of America;
> voted in favor of an amendment to cut foreign aid funds by $500,-000,000.

In 1951 Senator McCarthy

> voted in favor of a resolution to limit to four divisions the number of American troops the President could send to Europe without Congressional approval;
> voted in favor of an amendment to cut foreign aid funds by $300,-000,000;
> voted against increased funds for the government's information program;
> voted against ratification of the Japanese peace treaty (only nine other Senators joined him in this vote).

In 1952 Senator McCarthy

> voted in favor of an amendment to reduce Mutual Security fund authorization by $200,000,000;
> voted in favor of the McCarran-Walter immigration act;
> voted to pass the McCarran-Walter act over the President's veto.

In 1953 Senator McCarthy

> voted against an amendment to the Defense Department appropriation bill to increase funds for aircraft production by $400,000,000;
> voted against confirmation of Charles Bohlen as Ambassador to the Soviet Union;
> voted in favor of an amendment to cut military assistance funds for European allies by $500,000,000.

There was, then, a conspicuous turning point in McCarthy's voting record in 1950. What light did Senator McCarthy see in that year that made him change his position on the best means for achieving a strong and free democratic world — after his three years of silence on the

---

[3] At the time of writing, no important foreign policy votes had been recorded in 1954.

great anti-Communist developments of the post-war period?[4] After 1950, once McCarthy had adopted his new role, he found that his support had to come not from the Republican Party's internationalist wing but from its nationalist wing. Senators like Dirksen, Bridges, Welker, Bricker, and Jenner rallied to his support — and so he *quickly and conveniently abandoned his erstwhile internationalist friends, for whom he had been a minor figure, and joined forces with his new-found nationalist allies, who accepted him as their leader.*

This shift appears to have been dictated by cynical opportunism. McCarthy, of course, has no monopoly on political opportunism; but his shift does serve to reinforce skepticism about the sincerity and authenticity of his anti-Communist "crusade."

[4] In April 1950 McCarthy was asked, in the presence of Frederick Woltman, famous Pulitzer Prize-winning anti-Communist journalist: "Tell me, Senator, just how long ago did you discover Communism?" "Two and a half months!" replied the Senator.

G. David Schine—Authority on Communism

In February 1953, 26-year-old G. David Schine became chief consultant for the McCarthy subcommittee investigating Communist infiltration. His friend Roy Cohn, the subcommittee's chief counsel, has repeatedly stated — and during the Army-McCarthy hearings testified — that Schine is "very well versed on the subject of Communism."

What qualifications did Schine present in order to become the chief consultant to a committee purportedly looking for Communists? The only evidence publicly available to support his qualifications is a pamphlet, published in 1952, entitled *Definition of Communism*. It was printed in thousands of copies and placed in every room of the chain of hotels owned by the author's father.

An examination of this document is not irrelevant to the subject of of this book — McCarthy and the Communists. It is revealing in that it sheds light on the standards of knowledge and accuracy required of staff members of the McCarthy committee.

The analysis that follows is a summary of an article by William Caldwell, published in the May 24, 1953, issue of the *New Leader*, a publication that has been combatting Communism consistently, vigorously, and accurately for more than three decades and that has piled up an astonishing record of historically vindicated insight into public policy.

The Schine pamphlet consists of six small pages. It has six chapters, three of which are each one paragraph long.

1. Schine states unequivocally that "the theory of Communism was created by Marx in 1848."

This of course represents a gross historical inaccuracy concerning a philosophy to which many men contributed over a period of many years, before and after 1848. Schine apparently refers to *The Communist Manifesto*, which was published in that year. But several of Marx's basic tenets were expounded in such early writings as *The German Ideology* (1845-46), and some in books that appeared after 1848: *Das Kapital*, Vol. I (1867) and *Critique of the Gotha Program* (1875).

2. Schine states that "the Communist Party, its policies and procedures, were formulated by Nicolai Lenin in 1905."

The Communist Party as such did not exist until 1918. The Russian Social Democratic Labor Party, to which Schine seems to be referring, was the immediate precursor of the Communist Party. It formulated its statutes not in 1905 but at its Second Congress in 1903. Lenin, moreover, never used the name "Nicolai." He was always "Vladimir Ilyitch."

Furthermore Lenin did not by himself formulate the Party's statutes at that Congress. While the delegates generally adhered to his proposals, they also incorporated views that Lenin had violently opposed.

3. Schine refers to the "Russian Revolution of 1916." As a result of this Revolution, he informs us, the Tzarist government fell, and a Provisional Government "under the leadership of Kerensky" took its place.

There was no revolution in 1916. It took place in March 1917. The Provisional Government was first headed by Prince Lvov. Kerensky did not become premier until July of that year.

4. Schine states that Lenin evolved the first "series" of Five-Year Plans.

The "series" of Five-Year Plans began several years after Lenin's death in 1924, and the first such plan was drafted in 1927 and actually put into effect in 1928.

5. Schine states that "Joseph Stalin succeeded Nicolai Lenin in 1924."

Stalin succeeded Lenin. But from a historical point of view to state this is to explain nothing. Stalin had already become general secretary of the Communist Party before Lenin's death in 1924, and it was this position that he manipulated in his ultimately successful drive for total power. It was certainly not in this *position* that he succeeded Lenin, for the latter had never held it.

Nor did Stalin succeed to Lenin's *power* immediately after Lenin's death. It took at least three years of intense struggle among the top Bolshevik leaders before Stalin was able to consolidate his power, and it took a good many more years before he succeeded in eliminating all elements of potential rivalry and power-competition.

6. Schine states that Marx believed the revolution would eventually destroy capitalism and would institute a system of "State Socialism." This would create "a world in which there will be no materialism, no classes, and no unhappiness." Man would become "perfect," having no "aim in life other than the fulfillment of his material needs."

In the first place, this is clearly a misunderstanding of the philosophical term "materialism" and of Marx's interpretation of it. The gross oversimplification involved in Schine's use of the term consists in substituting the popular, vulgar connotation of the word for the rather complex instrument of historical-economic interpretation that Marx made of his "dialectical materialism." Also, Marx never envisioned "a world in which there will be no materialism," even in the popular sense of the word.

Finally, there is an inherent contradiction even in Schine's "explanation" of Marx's view: How is it possible for man to have no "aim in life other than the fulfillment of his material needs" in "a world in which there will be no materialism"?

7. *Schine states that "under Lenin's system [the one 'formulated . . . in 1905'] the Politburo, consisting of 12 men, was to rule the Communist party and, therefore, all of the Communist and Communist-dominated countries." As a later point, Mr. Schine goes on to list Austria as a Soviet satellite.*

The Politburo was not organized until 1917. Its number has never been fixed officially and has often varied.

Austria, of course, while it remains under Four-Power occupation, is far from being a Soviet satellite. Indeed, it is governed by an administration that has been vigorously and courageously anti-Communist.

In order to identify, pinpoint, and expose the Communist enemy, one must know and understand him. Proper intentions are not enough, nor are violent feelings. Full and accurate knowledge and understanding are the indispensable, initial weapons in the arsenal of the anti-Communist fight.

G. David Schine's pamphlet is characterized by numerous misstatements and misunderstandings. Surely these are not the qualifications for conducting an effective fight against Communism.

Index